Kid Cash

Creative money-making ideas

Joe Lamancusa

TAB Books
Division of McGraw-Hill, Inc.
Blue Ridge Summit, PA 17294-0850

Kid Cash

Creative money-making ideas

Dedication
To my mom.

Most mothers tell their kids
to go read a book when they're bored.
Mine told me to go write a book.
So I did!

Mom, the opportunities you propose to me
are ones that not many kids my age
get to experience.
All of your support and enthusiasm
toward whatever I do
gives me an even greater incentive to excel.
Even during my most trying times,
I look over and you're there with me
to support me, care for me, and love me.
Thank you for always being there.

I love you.

Acknowledgments
A very special thank you to the following people for helping to make this book a success:

My mother, Kathy Lamancusa
My father, Joe Lamancusa
Diane Soemisch
Kathleen Bretherick
Jim Lamancusa

Notices

Styrofoam is a registered trademark of Dow Chemical.
Creatively Yours is a registered trademark of Loctite Corporation.

FIRST EDITION
FIRST PRINTING

© 1993 by **Joe Lamancusa**.
Published by TAB Books.
TAB Books is a division of McGraw-Hill, Inc.

Library of Congress Cataloging-in-Publication Data
Lamancusa, Joe
  Kid cash : creative money-making ideas / by Joe Lamancusa
    p.   cm.
  Includes index.
    Summary: at least forty concrete, creative suggestions for ways to make money, with sample flyers for advertising oneself and information on setting fees, keeping records, and handling profits.
  ISBN 0-8306-4266-8 (hard)   ISBN 0-8306-4265-X (pbk.)
    1. New business enterprises—Juvenile literature. 2. Small business—Management—Juvenile literature. 3. Money-making projects for children—Juvenile literature. [1. Moneymaking projects. 2. Business enterprises.] I. Title.
  HD62.5.L35   1993   93-12502
  658'.041—dc20   CIP
                                           AC

Acquisitions Editor: Stacy Varavvas Pomeroy
Editorial team: Steve Bolt, Executive Editor
                Sally Anne Glover, Editor
Production team: Katherine G. Brown, Director
                Wanda S. Ditch, Layout
                Tina M. Sourbier, Typesetting
                Kelly Christman, Proofreading
Design team: Jaclyn J. Boone, Designer
                Brian Allison, Associate Designer
Cover design: Holberg Design, York, Pa.   KIDS

Contents

Introduction

How many times have you wished you had your own money that you could use for what you wanted? Well, money-making opportunities are lurking around every corner. It's just a matter of recognizing those opportunities and doing something about them. In this book, you'll find dozens of creative ideas for making money the old-fashioned way—by earning it!

I've been there, and know it can be very difficult to make money. A few years ago, I wanted to start babysitting to earn money. I mentioned to a few neighbors that I was available for hire. I didn't get a single call until I developed the babysitting flyer shown in this book. Within 24 hours of distributing the flyer, I had calls for more jobs than I could handle!

I've made it as easy as possible to read, understand, and get "million dollar" ideas from this book. It contains all kinds of jobs for all kinds of interests and skills. Each job is broken down into six easy-to-read sections:

☆ Job description—A brief explanation of the job and its responsibilities.
☆ Qualifications—Essential qualities, knowledge, and skills you must have in order to do the job well.
☆ Target customers—The people you should focus on to promote your job. For whom would you be doing this job? Children between certain ages, working parents, the elderly?
☆ Start-up costs—Anything you would need to purchase in order to complete the job, and approximately how much it would cost.
☆ Ideas for success—Further explanation of the responsibilities of the job and how to carry them out correctly. Special tips on how to do the job efficiently, creatively, and successfully. Warnings and safety precautions that should be taken before, during, and after doing a job.
☆ Suggested fees—A range of what you should charge for your services. You should think about this range and the amount of work you're doing for a person and come up with a reasonable,

exact fee within the range I've given. All costs that you encounter should be included in the fee. For some jobs, I suggest a flat rate (one fee for the entire job); for other jobs, I suggest an hourly rate.

In addition to the thorough job descriptions, *Kid Cash* provides a special feature that no other book of its kind does. For each job, you'll find a graphically illustrated flyer that advertises your specific service. The flyer has room for you to put your name and a little information about yourself. The special binding makes it simple to put this book on a photocopy machine and crank out as many copies as you want to distribute to all potential customers, including family, friends, neighbors, and local small business. Flyers are a concrete way to reach out to people and let them know that your service is available. After all, no business could exist without some form of successful advertising, and it doesn't get any easier than a ready-made flyer!

Instructions for copying and personalizing flyers are in chapter 42. Before reproducing any flyer, be sure to review its contents and see if you're willing to be responsible for all of the points spelled out on that particular flyer.

Starting your own small business and successfully and responsibly completing your job helps other people and brings you money! It also gives you a feeling of accomplishment and self-worth. Savor it. With that in mind, I'd like to sincerely wish you the best of luck in your endeavors, and I hope that you make a substantial amount of money. This can be a profitable and rewarding experience for you. So, above all else—have fun!

I'd love to hear about your successes in money making. If you've had any problems you'd like to share with others, I'd like to know that too, or if you have any questions about any of the material in this book, don't hesitate to write me at this address:

Joe Lamancusa
P.O. Box 2717
N. Canton, OH 44720

Good Luck!

caution symbols

You'll find caution symbols throughout this book to help you understand that you should take extra care when performing your jobs. Be sure to read over the explanations of each caution symbol so that you thoroughly understand what you're getting yourself into with each task.

Some of the jobs explained in this book require the use of sharp objects or flames or are potentially dangerous in other ways. You and a parent or other adult should carefully review each job you choose. All of the jobs in this book can be done safely, but you should take care with any potential areas of hazard that might be associated with each individual job. Thoroughly discuss these areas with a parent and understand what you will need to do to ensure safety for you and your customers.

For use as guides, the following symbols are placed in the upper outside corner of the page at the beginning of each job. Some children might be able to handle situations in a more mature manner than others, so parents/adults should use their good judgment as the final guide.

 Materials or tools used during this job could be dangerous in young hands. Adult supervision is recommended.

 You'll use a flame during this job. Don't wear loose clothing. Tie your hair back. Never leave a flame unattended, and, when you're through, extinguish the flame properly.

 You'll use a stove, boiling water, or other hot materials during this job, and only older children or adults should do this task. Keep small children away from boiling water and burners.

 You'll use electricity during this job. Adults should supervise young children and caution older children about the hazards of electricity.

 Adults should instruct children on the care and handling of sharp tools or combustible or toxic materials and how to protect themselves and others.

1
Babysitting

The need for good babysitters is growing fast, and you can help fill the demand!

job description   Caring for and entertaining children while their parents are away.

qualifications   You must be:

☆ Patient
☆ Understanding
☆ Fun
☆ Very responsible
☆ Prepared for all emergencies
☆ Open-minded

target customers   All families with children under the age of 11.

start-up costs   Duplication of flyers: $3 to $10.

ideas for success

1. Before babysitting for a new family, set up a time when you can meet with the parents and get to know the kids in advance.
2. Don't fall asleep on the job, even when the children are in bed.
3. Know where the parents are going to be and the phone numbers of those places.
4. Have all emergency phone numbers written down and nearby.
5. Don't be afraid to sit a child down if he or she is misbehaving.
6. When you're in doubt about a certain activity, don't do it!
7. Be aware of all family rules before the parents leave.

AVAILABLE

Excellent
Babysitter

Let Me Introduce Myself

- ❖ My name is **Joe Lamancusa.**
- ❖ I live at 7750 Gatewood Circle.
- ❖ I am 13 years old, (but will be 14 in January).
- ❖ I attend North Canton Middle School, 8th grade.
- ❖ I am active in the PANDA program (Prevent and Neutralize Drugs and Alcohol). This summer I served on the Youth Staff for the PANDA training.
- ❖ I am an honor student.
- ❖ I played young Ebeneezer Scrooge in the Canton Players Guilds' production of 'A Christmas Carol'; and the second lead role in 'A Thousand Clowns'.
- ❖ I am a member of Boy Scout troup 229.
- ❖ I am on the Academic Challenge Team.

I LOVE KIDS AND KIDS LOVE ME!!

Kids just melt in my arms!

Why you should hire me:

- ❖ I won't eat you out of house and home.

- ❖ I clean up after myself and the kids.

- ❖ Yes, I do change diapers.

- ❖ We have lots of fun.

- ❖ You won't come home to a ghastly mess.

- ❖ The kids will be in bed . . . . on time.

- ❖ I find your kids more interesting than your TV.

- ❖ They'll never miss you (well almost).

- ❖ I color, play blocks, ride bikes, teach them constructive and educational things, read bedtime stories, sing songs and do anything else they enjoy and YOU allow!

Next time you need an *Excellent Babysitter* - Call Joe

383-1166

AVAILABLE

Excellent
Babysitter

Let Me Introduce Myself

- ❖
- ❖
- ❖
- ❖
- ❖
- ❖

Kids just melt in my arms!

I LOVE KIDS AND KIDS LOVE ME!!

Why you should hire me:

- ❖ I won't eat you out of house and home.
- ❖ I clean up after myself and the kids.
- ❖ Yes, I do change diapers.
- ❖ We have lots of fun.
- ❖ I color, play blocks, ride bikes, teach them constructive and educational things, read bedtime stories, sing songs and do anything else they enjoy and YOU allow!
- ❖ You won't come home to a ghastly mess.
- ❖ The kids will be in bed . . .. on time.
- ❖ I find your kids more interesting than your TV.
- ❖ They'll never miss you (well, almost).

Next time you need an *Excellent Babysitter* - Call

8. Take complete phone messages, including the complete name of the caller, his or her phone number, and the time of the call.
9. If you're preparing a meal, know what the children are permitted to eat. Take all necessary precautions around stoves and electricity.
10. Don't give the children any medicine unless instructed by the parents.
11. Accidents can happen; don't leave a baby alone at any time.
12. Don't open the door for anyone.
13. Be sure you have a reliable ride home when the parents return.

suggested fees Let the parents bring up the subject of payment. Rates vary from area to area, from $1 to $3 per child per hour. Ask others what they charge for babysitting. Be reasonable!

2
Yard upkeep

If you enjoy the outdoors, yard upkeep is for you!

job description Maintaining lawns and greenery. Yard upkeep services include cutting grass, weeding gardens and flower beds, planting flowers, raking leaves, spreading mulch, and watering plants and lawns.

qualifications You must be:

☆ A fast and efficient worker
☆ Unafraid to get dirty
☆ Able to run a lawn mower and other motorized lawn tools
☆ Able to use tools, shovels, rakes, etc.

target customers Homeowners with yards.

start-up costs Duplication of flyers: $3 to $10. In some cases you'll have to provide the necessary tools and equipment for work; in other cases, your client will provide them.

ideas for success Before taking care of other people's yards, get some experience in maintaining your own yard. This will make your services all the more valuable to your customers.

Be flexible. Your client might want you to do a job that I haven't listed here. If you have the experience and know-how, do it! If it's a new task to you, explain that to your client and express an interest in learning, but ask the client to explain in detail what he or she wants done.

Yard Upkeep Service

* Is your yard getting out of control?
* Do you wish you could maintain your yard, but you don't have the time?

Well . . . yard upkeep is my specialty!!

About me:

*

*

*

*

*

*

*

Services offered:

* Lawn mowing.

* Weeding gardens.

* Flower planting.

* Leaf raking.

* Mulch or gravel spreading.

* Plant or grass watering.

* We can talk about other lawn needs you have.

Why you should hire me:

* I am a fast and efficient worker.

* I enjoy working outdoors.

* I'm not afraid to get dirty.

* I do a thorough job.

* I don't fool around; I WORK!

Next time you need help
with your <u>Yard Care</u>
Call

_____

_____

mowing lawns   Be safe with the lawn mower. Don't take any chances with safety. If you use a lawn mower without a bag, be sure to rake up all the grass clippings afterwards. The cost of your time to do this should be figured into the fees.

Always refill the gas tank after each cutting so it will be ready the next time you use it. It's a real pain to run out of gas in the middle of the job! If there are border areas or areas around plants or trees that you can't get with the lawn mower, use grass clippers or a weed whacker.

weeding gardens   Wear a pair of work gloves so you don't prick your fingers on thorns or sharp-edged leaves. If possible, use a tool called a weeder to aid you. This tool makes weeding so much easier.

The following is very important: Be sure to pull weeds out—roots and all! If you just snap the stem, the weed will be back up in no time and your client will be angry!

planting flowers or plants In addition to dirt already dug from the hole, put some rich, black, fertile soil in each of the holes as you plant. You or your client can purchase the soil, or find it near a stream or in the woods. This rich soil helps the flowers grow quickly.

Add any planting fertilizer that your client wishes. Be sure to have gloves on your hands and don't touch the fertilizer. Thoroughly water each flower or plant after planting. However, don't drown it.

Don't dig a hole too deep or too shallow. It should be deep enough to cover the plant's roots and shallow enough not to suffocate the flower. Check with your client to verify the depth that he or she wants them planted.

raking leaves Rake all the leaves into piles first, then put them in bags. If your client wants you to burn the leaves, check with your local city hall first. Burning leaves is illegal in some areas.

Be thorough. Rake leaves out of flower beds and gardens as well. Be careful not to damage the plants in the process.

spreading mulch or gravel A wheelbarrow is very helpful for carrying the mulch or gravel from the master pile to where it needs to go. Be sure to spread the mulch or gravel evenly and fully. A rake works best to spread the mulch. If there are any plants or flowers in the area you're to spread in, use your hands to carefully spread the mulch around the plant.

watering plants If you use a hose, stand back from the plants a few feet and don't use a hard stream of water. This protects the plants from being injured by the water. Remember, plants soak up water by their roots, not their leaves. Water toward the ground.

It's best not to water in the heat of the day, between 12:00 p.m. and 3:00 p.m., because the water will evaporate very quickly and might scorch the plants. Water early in the morning or later in the afternoon or evening.

suggested fees Discuss this with your client. Come up with either a flat rate or an hourly rate that you're both comfortable with. The fee should be determined by the size of the yard and how much work you'll be doing. Have a clear idea of how long it will take you to do what's being asked. Consult your friends who might be doing similar services in another area. They might be able to give you guidelines for your region.

3
Dog walking

A dog owner might not have time to handle all the care and attention a dog needs, so this job is for all you dog lovers out there.

job description Exercising other people's dogs by walking them around your neighborhood on a regular basis.

qualifications You must:

☆ Like dogs
☆ Be patient
☆ Be reasonably strong to maintain control of the dog
☆ Like to walk a fairly long distance
☆ Be responsible

target customers Anyone with a dog.

start-up costs Duplication of the flyers: $3 to $10.

ideas for success

1. Before you start walking the dog, set up times with the owner to let the dog get to know you. This will make it much easier when you do start walking the dog.
2. Never walk two dogs from different households at the same time.
3. Walk the dog thoroughly. Don't take short cuts. Give the dog all the exercise it needs.
4. Don't cut through other people's yards. The dog just might decide to go to the bathroom right there.

Excellent Dog Walker

➢ Is your dog too much to handle?
➢ Is your day so full that you don't even have time to do simple things like take your dog for a walk?

Well, I've got time!!

Who am I?

➢

➢

➢

You should hire me because:

➢ I love dogs and get along well with them.
➢ I am responsible and will take care of your dogs while I walk them.
➢ I can ease stress in your life by taking your dog off your hands for awhile.

Next time you need an
***Excellent Dog Walker* - Call**

5. Keep control of the dog at all times. Don't let it go into people's yards or into the middle of the street.
6. If there's a sidewalk in your neighborhood, walk the dog there instead of on the street.
7. You walk the dog; don't let the dog walk you. Plan out your route and stick to it.
8. Plan your trip so you don't walk by friends' (or enemies') houses. This could distract you from your job.

suggested fees Fees vary from area to area. I recommend charging between $1 and $3 per dog per walk. Discuss this with your client.

4
Potpourri hearts

Ah, Valentine's Day . . . when love is in the air . . . when Cupid's arrows are everywhere . . . the time when you're so excited to get that special valentine. Your excitement mounts; your heart's filled with joy as you open the envelope . . . and pull out the card. Augh! Ziggy again! Well, you can put a stop to those boring valentines that make you just want to puke!

Potpourri hearts are the perfect way to put some variety and excitement into Valentine's Day gifts. Guys, you can make this sweet-smelling gift for your sweetheart, and girls, if you have a special guy and you're thinking of making this for him . . . don't even think about it! Get him some candy! However, this is a great present for teachers and parents, and it doesn't take a lot of time, so you won't miss your favorite TV shows.

job description Making heart-shaped potpourri gifts and selling them.

qualifications You must:

☆ Enjoy working with your hands
☆ Be creative
☆ Be a precise worker—do the job right
☆ Enjoy "craft" projects

target customers Sentimental people of all ages who want to give the perfect Valentine's Day gift.

For Sale!

Beautiful
Potpourri Hearts

Give the gift of love this
Valentine's Day!

Only _____ each

Two for _____

* Great gift for your sweetheart.

* Decorate your house with the fragrance of
Valentine's Day.

If you are interested - Call:

At: _____

start-up costs Duplication of flyers: $3 to $10. Each finished heart will cost you between 50 cents and $1.

materials
- ☆ Potpourri of your choice. (I used Victorian Rose, approximately 2 ounces.)
- ☆ Heart-shaped, metal cookie cutter, 4 inches wide (any size and shape can be used. The finished piece will end up the size of the cookie cutter.
- ☆ One yard of ½-inch-wide picot-edged ribbon.
- ☆ One-half yard of 4mm fused pearls.
- ☆ White craft glue (I used Aleene's white tacky glue.)
- ☆ Craft cement (I used Creatively Yours Crafter's Cement.)
- ☆ Popsicle stick
- ☆ One 6-inch square of waxed paper
- ☆ Styrofoam cup
- ☆ Cooking spray
- ☆ Old, nonreusable bowl (Don't use a good bowl or your mom will kill you!)

instructions
1. Mix the potpourri. Fill the styrofoam cup to the top with potpourri and empty it into the bowl. Fill the styrofoam cup ⅓ full of white craft glue. It might seem like a lot, but you might have to add even more! With your popsicle stick, mix the glue and the potpourri together. If it gets hard to mix, add more glue. It will probably look like a big white mess, but don't worry; the glue will dry clear.
2. Prepare the cookie cutter. Lightly spray the inside of the cookie cutter and the top of the waxed paper with cooking spray. Place the cookie cutter on the waxed paper.
3. Form the Potpourri Heart. When the potpourri and the glue are well mixed and there are no big glue globs between the potpourri, place the mixture into the cookie cutter. Don't be afraid to get your hands in it; the glue just rubs right off. With your fingers and the popsicle stick, press the mixture evenly in the cookie cutter to fill any holes there might be.
4. Remove the heart from the cookie cutter. Wait 15 minutes. After 15 minutes it's very important that you take the potpourri out of the cookie cutter. Otherwise, the potpourri might stick to the cookie cutter, making it impossible to remove. When the mixture is removed from the cookie cutter, take a pencil and carefully poke a hole right below the "V" in the top of the

heart. Once removed, place the Potpourri Heart on the waxed paper and let it dry for 24–36 hours. Turn it over once in a while and it will dry more evenly.

5. Decorate the heart. When dry, apply craft cement to the side of the heart. Stick the ribbon to the glue and hold for a minute or so. Cut off the excess ribbon. Take a 9-inch piece of the additional picot-edged ribbon and stick it through the hole so that there's equal amounts of ribbon on either side of the hole. Tie two knots so the ribbon is tight around the hole. Bring the two ends of the ribbon up and together. Tie a knot at the ends to form a loop between the two knots. Form a bow with the other 9 inches of ribbon, just like you tie your shoe. Glue this bow to the front of the heart. Glue the fused pearls around the sides of the heart on top of the picot ribbon. Trim away any excess pearls.

Give this delightful present as a creative and different Valentine's Day gift.

other ideas
☆ Use smaller cookie cutters to make mini-hearts. The mixture described in this chapter will make two 2-inch hearts.
☆ Add a magnet to the back so this can be displayed on a refrigerator or other piece of metal.
☆ Raid your mother's crafting boxes and use scraps of flowers, ribbons, and whatever else you can find to decorate the hearts. (Ask Mom first!)

ideas for success
1. All the supplies you need for this project should be a carried by your local craft store. Check there first.
2. Before buying brand new cookie cutters, check around your kitchen. Chances are you'll find some there. However, remember to wash them very well with hot water and soap after you're finished.
3. The potpourri doesn't have to be heart shaped. Use different cookie cutters for different shapes.
4. Use your imagination in decorating the potpourri hearts. Remember, these are going to people as gifts, so make them as special as you can.
5. If you have a sweetheart of your own, give him or her one of these.

6. A few days after you've delivered your flyers, you might want to go door to door with a finished heart to show your neighbors what they would be getting.

suggested fee Charge between $2 and $4 per heart.

5
Tree decorating

Every family wants a beautiful tree at Christmas time, but do they have the time to decorate it?

job description
Decorating other people's Christmas trees with their lights and ornaments, and possibly taking them down again when the season is over.

qualifications
You must:

☆ Be a good worker
☆ Have respect for other people's property
☆ Have that "decorative" touch
☆ Want to bring Christmas joy to others
☆ Be responsible

target customers
Adults/parents with Christmas trees. The elderly.

start-up costs
Duplication of flyers: $3 to $10.

ideas for success
1. Get the flyers out well before Christmas (the end of November—no later than the beginning of December). Busy people who were otherwise not going to buy a tree might reconsider.
2. Don't use your own ornaments. Number one, you'd have to carry them to your client's house. Number two, while you're away, your client might like them so much, he or she would keep one or two (you never know).
3. Always put the lights on the tree first.
4. Work with what you have. If fewer ornaments are available, evenly space them farther apart so the tree looks balanced. Fill the entire tree.

Oh, Christmas Tree
Oh, Christmas Tree

Don't have time to decorate your Christmas tree?
Let me do it for you!

* A nicely decorated tree is something that shouldn't be overlooked just because you don't have time.

* You supply the ornaments; I supply the time!

Call _____ at _____ for Christmas
Cheer and a decorated tree too!

5. Tinsel isn't very expensive—50 cents to $2. You might want to bring some tinsel over as a little bonus. This will show your client that you're serious about this, yet giving. However, check with your client to see if they want tinsel.
6. Remember, the better job you do, the more likely your client is to ask you back next year.
7. When taking the ornaments down, be sure to pack them neatly in the boxes they came in so they'll survive the year of storage without cracks and breaks.
8. Always take the lights off last.
9. Double and triple check that you didn't leave any ornaments on the tree. Sometimes they can hide pretty well!

suggested fee Depending on the size of the tree and the amount of decorations you have to put on, I would charge between $10 and $15 per tree.

6
Odd-job service

People often ignore and put off the little tasks, but you can do them!

job description Doing little jobs around the house for your neighbors. Tasks could include: dishes, laundry, sweeping, weeding, watering, and little fix-it jobs.

qualifications You must be:

☆ Good with tools
☆ Handy with many jobs around the house
☆ A hard, meticulous worker
☆ A do-the-job-right type of person
☆ Able to work within guidelines given by the client

target customer Busy, working homeowners. Older or disabled homeowners.

start-up costs Duplication of flyers: $3 to $10.

ideas for success
1. If you need any cleaning agents such as soaps, see if your client can provide those because they'll drive up your expenses.
2. If you have to purchase a tool especially for a job, be sure to add that to your fee.
3. I've listed several "odd jobs" that can be part of your service. If you think of another job you want to offer or if your client has a special request, do it!
4. "Odd jobs" can be anything from little tasks to time-consuming repairs. Know what you're getting into before you make the commitment. Yet, let your clients know what you can and can't do.

Having trouble getting the little things done?

Why not have my

<u>Odd-Job Service</u>

do them for you?

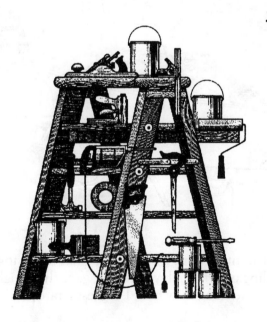

<u>Services performed:</u>

* Fix-it type jobs
*Washing dishes
* Doing laundry
* Sweeping and washing floors
* Weeding gardens
* Watering gardens and flowers
* Any other service you need me to do!

Call _____ **at** _____
to get the little things done!

5. If you don't know how to do a job requested by your client, say
so! Don't wing it and make the situation worse.

suggested fees Your clients might want to work with you on a flat rate (single
payment), depending on what job you're doing, or they might
want to pay you by the hour, for which I suggest a rate of $1 to $3
per hour.

7
Car wash

There are a whole lot of dirty cars near you, and you can wash a lot of them!

job description Washing/waxing other people's cars, vans, bikes, or boats.

qualifications You should:

☆ Not mind getting wet
☆ Be a hard worker
☆ Be attentive to detail
☆ Not be allergic to any car soaps or waxes

target customers Anyone with a car, bike, van, or boat. Elderly car owners who can't wash cars themselves.

start-up costs Duplication of flyers: $3 to $10. Car soap, car wax, sponges, glass cleaner, bucket, paper towels, and towels or rags for drying.

ideas for success
1. Put a glob of soap about the size of a half dollar in the bucket before you fill it with water.
2. Use lukewarm water—not too hot, not too cold.
3. Wash the car in sections, wetting each section with the hose before you wash. Rinse each section with the hose after you wash it.
4. It's very important to dry the vehicle with towels or rags immediately after you wash. Otherwise, the water will sun dry and leave ugly spots.
5. When drying, don't forget to get the inside edges of all the doors, including the trunk. Water sometimes seeps in through the cracks.

How long has it been since your car has been thoroughly washed?

Get a thorough

Car Wash

from me!

* One-time or regular car washes available.

* I wax upon request.

* I do windows inside and out!

Never let your car go dirty again!

Call _____ **at** _____

for spotless cars!

6. After drying, go back and wash all windows, inside and out, with a glass cleaner.
7. Check in your garage or laundry room closet for supplies. You'd be surprised at what you have around the house.
8. Bring all of your own supplies. This is less hassle for the car owners and for you, but fill the bucket with water after you get there.
9. Follow the directions on the wax bottle exactly.
10. On bikes, use chrome polish for the metal to get it nice and shiny!
11. The better job you do this time, the more likely you are to be asked back again!
12. About a week after delivering the flyers, go door to door with all your supplies and dressed to work. Someone might just hire you on the spot!

suggested fees Have several rates available for different wash and wax jobs. I suggest between $3 and $5 per car—higher rates, between $7 and $15, for trucks and vans. Boat sizes vary greatly. Use your own judgment, based on what you charge for car washes.

8
Pet sitting

If you love animals, this job is for you!

job description Taking care of pets for short or long periods of time while the owners are away.

qualifications You must:

☆ Love animals
☆ Not be allergic to animals
☆ Be responsible
☆ Be patient
☆ Have time to devote to pets

target customers Anyone, adult or child, with any kind of pet.

start-up costs Duplication of flyers: $3 to $10.

ideas for success
1. Household pets range from ants to snakes. Each requires different care. Be sure you know how to care for an animal before you accept the job.
2. Pet food is almost as varied as human food. To save you a lot of hassle and money, require your client to provide the food— enough for the entire time you're responsible for the animal.
3. Pet sitting can mean going over to your client's house a few times a day, or housing the pet in your own home. Be prepared for either option.
4. Be sure to receive clear instructions from your client regarding what kind of care the pet requires, feeding times, and any special instructions. This will make caring for the pet easier.

Available

Petsitter

Why you should hire me:

* I love animals.

* I am responsible and caring.

* Your pet is my top priority.

* I follow special care instructions to the letter.

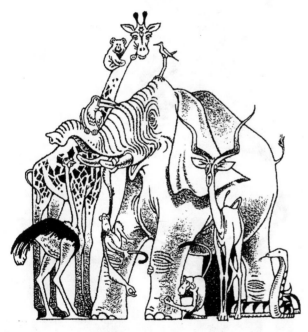

You can trust me with your pet!

Call _____ at _____
for a responsible petsitter.

5. The pet is your responsibility. If the pet makes a mess, you clean it up.

suggested fees Fees for this job depend on the amount of time you take care of the pet. If you care for the pet at your house, I recommend between $1.50 and $3.00 per day. If you're only going over to their house a few times a day, 50 cents to $1.50 is sensible.

9
Vacation services

Several jobs relating to home, yard, and pet care can be combined into one big job called "vacation services."

job description This job requires you to go over to a vacationing client's house and do small jobs to keep everything under control.

qualifications You must be:

☆ Reliable and responsible
☆ Efficient
☆ Able to do a variety of jobs

target customers Adults in your neighborhood.

start-up costs Duplication of flyers: $3 to $10.

ideas for success
1. Refer to the following jobs, which are also described in this book: yard upkeep, pet sitting, lawn mowing, leaf raking, mail retrieving, trash collecting, and plant sitting.
2. Don't forget to show up for a job at your client's house at the designated time. It might be very important that it's done on time.
3. Keep your options open. If your client has a special request, do your best to fill it.

Vacation Services

Are you going away for business or pleasure?
Have me take care of your home while you are away.

Services:

* Yard Upkeep

* Pet Sitting

* Lawn Mowing

* Leaf Raking

* Mail Retrieval

* Trash Collecting

* Plant Sitting

And whatever else is

needed

Call _____ at _____
for any needed Vacation Services

suggested fees I recommend a daily rate based on how much you're required to do. Base this fee on the "suggested fees" section of the jobs listed in the "ideas for success" section of this chapter.

10

Compile recipe books

People are always dying to try out new recipes, and you can sell them!

job description Collecting recipes from your parents, family, friends, and neighbors, putting the recipes all in a book, and selling them to avid cooks.

qualifications You must have:

☆ Neat, legible handwriting or access to a computer or typewriter
☆ Some relatives that like to cook

target customers People who enjoy cooking.

start-up costs Duplication of flyers and recipes: $3 to $10.

ideas for success
1. Keep all the page sizes uniform. If, when you are done collecting your recipes, you find that all of them are reasonably short, then half sheets of paper are adequate. However, if even a few recipes are longer, make them all full pages.
2. There are several ways of presenting the recipes. The papers can be stapled together in booklet form or compiled in a folder, but remember, a folder is an extra cost.
3. If you think of a clever way to present the recipes, do it!
4. If you have access to one, do your recipes on a computer or typewriter for a neater, more professional look.
5. Don't use a pencil on your final "for sale" model. If you have orders for several books, rather than writing each one out, photocopy all pages so the job goes faster. Include the price of photocopying in the price of the book.

Looking for new recipes to make for family, friends or guests?

Try one of my

Recipe Books

<u>Contains recipes in the areas of:</u>
* Drinks / Punches
* Desserts
* Entrees
* Vegetables
* Ethnic foods
* Appetizers

Cook up something new tonight!

Call _____ at _____

for great new culinery delights!

suggested fees Depending on the number of pages in the recipe book, between $5 and $10 per book is adequate.

11
Snow shoveling

Snow shoveling is a highly demanded service, and every snowfall is another business opportunity!

job description Shoveling snow off people's driveways and walkways to make room for vehicles and feet that don't want to get wet.

qualifications You must be:

☆ Unafraid of the cold
☆ Fairly strong and durable
☆ Willing to start and finish the job

target customers Small businesses who have areas to be shoveled. Adults who own homes (and have a driveway). Older people who can't shovel.

start-up costs Duplication of flyers: $3 to $10.

ideas for success
1. To make the job easier, clear one strip right in the center of the driveway from the top to the bottom, then shovel the snow off in rows from the center, doing each side separately.
2. Use your client's snow shovels at first. Later, if business is really booming, you might want to invest in your own snow shovel. Your client might also want you to salt the driveway to get rid of any ice that's hard to shovel. There are a few proper ways to apply salt. One, cut a hole in a plastic milk jug, scoop up the salt, and evenly shake it on the driveway; or two, wearing a pair of thick work gloves, throw the salt on evenly by hand. Whichever way you decide to do it, be sure to wear gloves at all times. I also recommend that you require your client to provide the salt. This will save you from having to carry it over (salt is

Let it snow, let it snow, let it snow . . . .

Don't have time to shovel your own driveway?
Let me do it for you!

Snow Shoveling Service

* I come upon request,
   anytime you need me.

* I am very thorough.

* I make sure to shovel
   walkways and porches.

Don't get snowed in this winter!

Call _____ at _____
for snow-free driveways - all the time!

heavy!), and it gives your client the chance to buy the kind that he or she wants.

3. Shovel off your client's walkways to doors, steps, and stoops as an added "extra." This makes the client more likely to ask you back again.

4. Shovel the drive completely. Don't leave any strips or piles of snow. The neater the job, the better.

5. You or your client might have access to a snow blower. This works a great deal faster, but be sure you know how to operate it.

suggested fees Many people will pay you quite well for doing this hard and time-consuming job. My suggested range is between $5 and $7 for a regular-sized driveway. Charge a few dollars extra for long or circular driveways.

12
Golf caddie

If there are any golf courses near you, chances are there's also a demand for caddies.

job description
Carrying your client's golf bag and clubs around the course with him or her. Assisting your client with the game by spotting and fetching balls, setting tees, and washing balls.

qualifications
You must be:

☆ Able to walk a very long way while carrying golf clubs
☆ Fairly knowledgeable about the game of golf
☆ Patient with and respectful of other people
☆ Responsible
☆ Reasonably strong

target customers
Anyone who golfs.

start-up costs
Duplication of flyers: $3 to $10.

ideas for success
1. Check with your local golf course. They might already have a caddying program that you can get involved with.
2. In addition to delivering your flyers to houses, put a stack in the club house of a nearby golf course for golfers to pick up. Get permission from the course management first.
3. Spend time at the golf course handing out flyers. If someone is in need of a caddie, he or she might hire you on the spot!
4. Be familiar with manners and etiquette on a golf course so you won't disrupt the play of your client and others.
5. When someone yells fore, duck!

FORE!
Golf Caddie
Available

* I carry your bag.

* I shag your balls.

* I wash and spot your balls.

* I yell "fore."

* I take the blame for bad shots.

* I applaud you on the good shots.

Don't go 18 or even 9 without me at your side!

**Call _____ at _____
for caddying services that are hole-in-one quality!**

suggested fees This job is paid for by the hour. I recommend charging between $3 and $5 per hour.

13
Recyclable materials collector

Recycling is becoming more and more popular every day, and it just might be our only hope for the future. Here's how you can help.

job description
Collecting bags of aluminum, glass, plastic, and paper compiled by other people, then taking the materials to your local recycling drop-off areas.

qualifications
You must:

☆ Be interested in saving the earth
☆ Have a recycling drop-off near you and a way to get there

target customers
All neighbors and friends, whether they recycle or not.

start-up costs
Duplication of flyers: $3 to $10.

ideas for success
1. Deliver the flyers to people you know who recycle, but also give the flyers to people who don't recycle. If they know you would collect their recyclables and they wouldn't have to take the time to deliver the materials to a drop-off, they might take up recycling.
2. By asking your clients to put their recyclables in garbage bags according to material, you'd be saving time, and the recyclables would be easier to transport.
3. Start a recycling program in your own home. It's your way of helping the environment!
4. Check with your local recycling drop-off; some areas will pay you per bag that you deliver. That's extra income!

Do you recycle?

Do you think it is a pain to deliver your materials to a recycling drop?

Well, with me as your . . .

Recyclable Materials Collector

you'll never have to drop them off again!

I pick your recyclables up from your house and deliver them to the local drop-off for you.

Preserving the planet can be much easier for you.

Call _____ at _____

to collect your recyclables.

suggested fees The easiest way to get paid for this job is to charge by the bag. A reasonable rate is 50 cents to $1 per bag.

14
Mass mailings

Mass mailing is a very demanding, time-consuming job, but it can also be very profitable!

job description
Businesses often mail information to 500 people or more. Each one of those envelopes has to have the right papers put into it and be labeled, sealed, and stamped. This is a job for you!

qualifications
You must be:

☆ Very patient
☆ An efficient worker
☆ Meticulous—put the right papers in the right places
☆ Able to sit for a long period of time

target customers
Small businesses or home businesses that either send mailings or prepare them. Local mid-sized businesses.

start-up costs
Duplication of flyers: $3 to $10.

ideas for success
1. Start an assembly line. Lay out all the stacks of paper in a row in order. Then, just take one piece of paper from the top of each stack and put the papers in the envelope.
2. Don't do the entire process at once. First, gather and fold all the inserts. Then stuff the envelopes. Then seal them. Then stamp them. This saves time in the long run.
3. Play some music or watch something while you work. This will make the time seem to go by faster. If all else fails, whistle while you work!
4. Know how your client wants the job done. A certain order of papers can be very important.
5. Get in touch with your client concerning where the job is to be done. In some cases, he or she might bring the materials to your

Need help with your
Mailings?

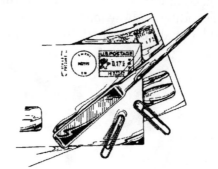

* Mass Mail Preparations

* Collating

* Envelope Stuffing

* Stamping

* Label Preparation

Don't tackle the horrendous job of your mailings by yourself.

Call _____ **at** _____

for efficient service!

5. Get in touch with your client concerning where the job is to be done. In some cases, he or she might bring the materials to your house; in other cases, you might have to go to an office or home.
6. Offer to take all the finished envelopes directly to the post office and mail them. This will save your client time and earn you more money.

suggested fees Discuss your payment with your client. The standard method of payment for this type of job is a set rate per envelope or unit that you complete, times the number that you do. However, this varies depending on how many items have to go in one envelope. Also, add a small fee if you deliver the mailing to the post office.

15
Lawn mowing

Imagine what the yards in your neighborhood would look like if they were never cut. You'd live in a jungle!

job description Using a push mower or a riding lawn mower to cut other people's grass. Trimming around tight edges with clippers or a trimmer. Raking the cut grass and disposing of it properly.

qualifications You must:

☆ Know how to safely operate a lawn mower or tractor
☆ Not be allergic to any grasses or weeds
☆ Be an efficient and fairly strong worker
☆ Enjoy the outdoors

target customers Businesses with lawns, all homeowners with yards that need to be cut, and elderly homeowners who can't mow the lawn themselves.

start-up costs Duplication of flyers: $3 to $10. Lawn mower, rake, gas.

ideas for success
1. Before doing other people's yards, practice on your own yard to gain experience.
2. When you're just starting out, use borrowed equipment from your client or your home. As your business grows, you might want to purchase your own equipment.
3. Be dependable. Establish a certain time during the week to do a lawn and be sure to come back around that time each week so your client knows when to expect you.
4. Mow in neat rows. Your path can often be seen when you're finished. No one wants zig-zags in the yard!

Imagine the jungle you'd live in if your grass was never cut!

Take advantage of my

Lawn Mowing

services to keep your yard under control.

* Weekly and one-time schedules available.

* I trim edges.

* I rake up excess grass if needed.

Don't get caught in your jungle . . .

Call _____ **at** _____

for reliable lawn mowing services

5. Always rake grass clippings from yards if your mower doesn't have a bag. Be sure to sweep up any clippings blown into driveways, streets, or sidewalks. A neat job is a better job!
6. Trim the grass near buildings, houses, or flower beds with an electric trimmer or hand clippers.
7. Businesses often have a vast amount of property. Don't forget about them.

suggested fees   It's difficult to set any one certain fee for this type of job, due to the fact that yards are so many different sizes. Check with friends and neighbors for the going rate in your area. Your clients might already have a certain price range in mind. Discuss it with them one on one.

16
Computer services

If you're skilled in operating a computer, this job is right up your alley!

job description
Computer services are in great demand. Local neighborhood organizations and family or small businesses need services such as typing up local or school newsletters, homemade invitations, mailings, or labels.

qualifications
You must:

☆ Know how to operate computer equipment efficiently and safely
☆ Have sufficient typing skills
☆ Have access to a computer and printer

target customers
Local organizations that put out typed information, small businesses in your area, and adults who need services for their business or school.

start-up costs
Duplication of flyers: $3 to $10. Computer paper: $2.50 to $3.50 for 500 sheets.

ideas for success
1. If you have a real interest in computers but can't type very well, you might want to take a typing course. You'll definitely need this skill in the future, so why not learn it now?
2. If you have cheap access to a copy machine, you might also offer to duplicate what you've typed.
3. Computers aren't toys. Be sure to operate all equipment safely and responsibly.

Computer Services

Available

Services professionally performed and creatively produced.

* Newsletters
* Invitations
* Labels
* Flyers
* Announcements
* . . . whatever else you need!

Save your time and still get a quality product in return!

Call _____ **at** _____

to serve your computer needs.

4. Once your business gets going, you might want to look into a computer class to sharpen your knowledge and teach you how to better use your computer. Be sure to check that the class teaches with the kind of computer you have. The better you know your computer, the more creative you can be with your job.
5. This job could be added to the service of mass mailing. After you're finished typing the information, stuff it in envelopes, stamp it, and send it!

suggested fees Have one set fee per page. An acceptable range is between $5 and $15, depending on what your client wants you to do. If your computer has any artistic or graphic capabilities, offer them. Charge between $3 and $5 per extra illustration or graphic.

17
Clowning around

Younger kids love clowns, and parents will pay well for entertainment that keeps children quiet!

job description Dressing up as a clown and entertaining at children's birthday parties. Doing tricks and funny acts to make kids laugh.

qualifications You must:

☆ Have a wild and zany personality with lots of creativity
☆ Know some magic or entertaining tricks
☆ Love little kids
☆ Be able to make up your own "clowning" tricks

target customers Families with kids between the ages of three and nine and families with two working parents who don't have much time to plan a party. Single parent households where the parent needs help due to lack of time and lack of support.

start-up costs Duplication of flyers: $3 to $10, clown suit with wig: $30 to $40, makeup: $2 to $4.

ideas for success
1. Check around your house for any clowning supplies such as magic kits, clown suits, or makeup. Try to save money whenever you can.
2. Be creative and make up your own act to entertain the kids. The more original, the better. Remember, kids love corny stuff!
3. Additional clown supplies include balloons, candy, and long balloons for making balloon animals. Anything you can use to improve your act is worth the few dollars it costs to buy it. Kids like to see things. The more objects you have, the better.
4. If you're skilled in sewing, it will be cheaper to buy fabric and make your own clown costume.

Having a birthday party for your child?

Let me entertain the kids by being a

Party Clown

* Magic Tricks   * Gift Bags

* Clowning Acts   * Games

* Audience Participation Activities

Give your child the funniest party ever!

Call _____ at _____
for clowning-around fun at your child's birthday

5. Make your show as jam-packed with funny stuff as you can. The more you make the kids laugh, the more likely the parent will be to ask you to return, or recommend you to friends.

6. If possible, learn how to make balloon animals. This is one of the most popular tricks with kids. Then the kids will have something to take home to remember you by. You can find books on this at your local library.

7. Make a good impression on the kids. If they like you, they might go home and tell their parents about you, and you might get another job out of it.

8. Above all, have fun. Also be sure that the kids have fun. Never forget that you're a full-fledged clown!

suggested fees The average birthday party lasts about two hours. I recommend charging between $10 and $20 per hour. That's some quick cash!

18
Leaf raking

It's totally unavoidable: The leaves will fall when autumn comes. Here's your chance to take advantage of this natural occurrence!

job description Raking leaves out of other people's yards and disposing of the leaves properly.

qualifications You must:

- ☆ Not be allergic to any grasses or leaves
- ☆ Have a strong back and strong arms
- ☆ Be thorough—do the whole job

target customers Local businesses with trees, homeowners who have yards with trees, and elderly people who are unable to rake leaves themselves.

start-up costs Duplication of flyers: $3 to $10.

ideas for success
1. To begin your business, you might want to use a borrowed rake from home (with mom and dad's permission). Once your business takes off and is doing well, buying your own rake would be sensible.
2. If your business gets so big that you just don't know what to do with all the money, you might look into buying a leaf blower. One of these would make your job much faster and easier. However, take into account that you've added an extra cost with gas to power the blower—unless it's an electric blower, in which case you'll need a long extension cord.
3. If there's a wooded area owned by your client, you can rake the leaves into the woods, and they'll safely decompose. If no wooded area is available, packing the leaves tightly in garbage bags is another way of disposing of the leaves. However, check

Piles and piles of leaves covering your yard, walk, and flower beds?

Take advantage of my
Leaf Raking Service

* Weekly and one-time schedules available.

* I rake out flower beds.

* I dispose of your leaves in the manner you wish.

Don't lose the battle against falling leaves!

**Call _____ at _____
to get rid of all your leaves - all season!**

your city's laws regarding disposal of leaves to make sure what's legal in your area.

4. Rake leaves off bushes and out of flower beds as well, being careful not to damage any plants.

5. Do a complete job. Don't leave large amounts of leaves scattered throughout the yard.

6. Check back with your client periodically throughout the season to see if they would like their yard raked again.

7. A few days after delivering your flyers, go to the doors of the houses you delivered to and remind them that you provide this service. Be sure to be polite and introduce yourself, and they might hire you on the spot!

8. Don't forget local businesses. They need your help, too!!

suggested fees A flat rate per half acre of yard is the best way to charge for this job. I would charge between $5 and $7 per half acre. Discuss this measurement with your client to estimate the size of their yard. This rate would also apply to business yards. They're usually measured in exact acreage, so pricing will be easy there.

19
Birthday parties

By planning other people's birthday parties, you'll be planning profits for yourself.

job description Completely planning birthday parties for younger children, including invitations, food, games, prizes, and decorations. Setting up before the party, staying through to run things, and staying after to clean up.

qualifications You must be:

☆ Creative and fond of younger kids
☆ A good planner (thorough)
☆ Dedicated
☆ Sociable towards kids and adults

target customers Parents with kids between the ages of five and ten, families with two working parents who don't have time to plan a party, single parent households where the parent needs help.

start-up costs Duplication of flyers: $3 to $10. Be flexible and work with all kinds of budgets. Costs for this job will include invitations, food, game supplies, eating utensils, prizes, and decorations. All of these together will cost about $40, with slight variations due to specific product pricing. However, don't let this figure scare you. Your customer will reimburse you for expenses.

Don't have time to plan your child's
Birthday Party?
Have me do it for you!

Birthday Party Planner

You don't have to do a thing! I plan and DO everything.

* Invitations
* Food
* Games
* Prizes
* Decorations
* Gift Bags
* Setup beforehand
* Cleanup afterward

Give your child a party to remember!

Call _____ at _____
for Birthday Party planning at its best!

ideas for success

1. Set up a meeting with the parents at least three weeks before the party. Discuss things such as date and time, what food to have, what games will be appropriate, and the theme of the party. Take careful, detailed notes. Prepare a list of about twenty different party themes they can choose from. Some popular themes include race cars, horses, flowers, sports, video games, outer space, and popular cartoon characters such as Garfield, Disney, and Barbie. Consult the parents about the child's individual interests and try to include as many of them as possible. Ask for an advance payment of approximately $40 to buy supplies. Save all receipts and any change to return to your customer.

2. Send invitations out at least two weeks before the party. Instruct the guests to RSVP to the birthday child's parents, but instruct the parents to notify you if anyone can't come.

3. Take into account whether this party is for a boy or a girl, and pick appropriate decoration colors.

4. Decorations include balloons, streamers, and signs. Use creativity and variety when decorating for a party. If possible, use the favorite color of the birthday child.

5. Many gift and party supply stores have complete sets of plastic silverware, paper, invitations, paper plates, paper cups, and napkins with popular party themes printed on them. Consult these places when making your theme list.

6. The party clown job (chapter 17) can be combined here as an added service. You can be a clown for the party you planned.

7. Make something that the kids can take home, such as a gift bag. Gift bags could include balloons, a party hat, a noisemaker, crayons, a coloring book, masks, etc., and, of course, put one of your "party planner" flyers in each bag (for the kids to show their parents). This is free advertising, and if the kids liked you, they might have you plan their party.

8. Having games means having prizes for the winners. Good prizes include candy, crayons or markers, coloring books, and balloons.

9. As for choosing a birthday cake, get an appropriate size for the number of kids attending the party. Get the favorite flavor of the birthday child, and have it decorated according to the theme chosen. To save money, you could make and decorate the cake yourself.

10. Arrive at least half an hour before the party starts to set up games, food, and decorations. Thoroughly clean up after the party, properly disposing of trash.
11. Make a complete list of everything you need for the party. As you secure an item, cross it off in your notes. The more organized you are, the better.
12. Read additional information in party books.

Once again, the complete list of things to consider when planning a birthday party:

☆ Date and time
☆ Number of children
☆ What food to have
☆ Theme of party
☆ Setup beforehand
☆ Invitations
☆ Eating utensils
☆ Cake (favorite flavor of birthday child)
☆ Decorations (favorite colors of birthday child)
☆ Games
☆ Cleanup afterward
☆ Appropriate prizes
☆ Gift bags (include your flyer)
☆ Meeting beforehand (careful notes)
☆ Boy or girl?
☆ Entertain as clown? (chapter 17)

suggested fees I recommend charging between $6 and $10 per child. Charge nothing for the birthday child, depending on how costly your expenses are. Collect half of the money ahead of time at the meeting. You'll need this for supplies and food. Collect the rest after the party. This can be a pretty hefty profit, but watch your expenses!

20
Gift wrapping

The better you wrap, the harder it is to guess what the gift is. That's the gift-giving spirit!

job description — Wrapping other people's gifts for all occasions, such as: Christmas, birthdays, Easter.

qualifications — You must:

☆ Be a neat and fast worker
☆ Know how to properly wrap all kinds of packages (circular, square, rectangular, triangular)
☆ Have the true spirit of gift giving

target customers — Children who can't wrap a present themselves, but can't let their parents wrap it because the gift is for their parents; people of all ages (2 to 102) who give gifts for special occasions; businesses who give employee gifts and can't ask any of their employees to wrap them.

start-up costs — Duplication of flyers: $3 to $10; wrapping paper: $2 to $4 per 50 square feet; stick-on bows: 5 and 10 cents apiece; tape: $1 to $2 per roll; scissors (find some around the house).

ideas for success —
1. There are many books on gift wrapping. Read up and get creative with your wrapping.
2. Clear tape comes in multiple packs of three or more. Purchase tape this way and save money in the long run.

Have gifts that need to be wrapped?

Try my speedy:

Gift Wrapping Service

Let me make it easy on you!

* I wrap all package shapes.

* I use ribbon and bows
   upon request.

* Holiday, Birthday or
   Special Day -
   I wrap them all!

After all, it is more fun if they don't know what's in it,

Right?

Call _____ **at** _____

for gift wrapping today!

3. Christmas will obviously be your biggest time of the year. With permission from the management, you can set up a gift wrapping table at a local mall. They might charge you a small fee to set up there, but with all the shoppers out there that need gifts wrapped, it's well worth it!
4. Deliver flyers several times a year near the holidays to remind people that you're still available.
5. Stick a bow on every package as an added extra for looks.

suggested fees Have several fees for different-sized boxes. Make a price chart with exact prices, similar to the one in TABLE 20-1.

SIZE	PRICE per package
SMALL (jewelry-size box)	.50 - $1.00
MEDIUM	$1.00 - $2.00
LARGE (clothing box)	$2.00 - $3.00
X-LARGE (larger than clothing box)	$3.00 - $5.00

21
Gathering firewood

Stoke up the fire for winter warmth!

job description
Gathering and/or stacking firewood for others. You might also incorporate coming back and restocking an on-hand supply indoors every so often.

qualifications
You must be:

☆ Strong
☆ Efficient

target customers
Homeowners who have or need firewood, elderly persons who can't handle their own firewood.

start-up costs
Duplication of flyers: $3 to $10.

ideas for success
1. If you have to transport the firewood from one place to another before you stack it, a wheelbarrow is very handy. It wouldn't be worth your while to buy one, so look into borrowing one from a friend or renting one.
2. Just because firewood is only used in winter, that doesn't mean you have to work then. If your client has the wood already, stack it as soon as possible, before it gets cold outside. It's no fun working when it's freezing.

Available
Firewood Stacker

* **Strong**

* **Hard Worker**

* **Dedicated**

**If you have firewood,
I'll stack it!**

Call _____ at _____
for more info about my firewood stacking service that <u>you</u> <u>need</u>!

suggested fees The way to charge for this job is by the size of stack you make. A *cord* is a stack of wood that's 4 feet wide by 4 feet tall by 8 feet long. A *rick* is a stack of wood that's 2 feet wide by 2 feet tall by 8 feet long. I recommend charging between $9 and $12 per cord and $3 to $6 per rick. If the stack of wood is smaller than that, use your own judgment, based on these prices.

22
Window washer

Everyone hates doing windows, and people will pay handsomely to get someone else to do them. That someone else should be you!

job description Throughly washing other people's windows and washing screens for windows, if requested.

qualifications You must:

☆ Like to wash windows
☆ Be thorough—do the job correctly and completely

target customers People who own houses with windows (most people), the elderly, and local businesses and establishments located in buildings with windows.

start-up costs Duplication of flyers: $3 to $10. Glass cleaner: approximately $2.75.

ideas for success
1. Instead of paper towels, it's better to use cloth towels and rags to wash windows. Rags and towels are softer and last much longer. I'll bet there are some old towels or rags hiding around your house. Hunt them down and use them!
2. If requested, wash both sides of the windows. This looks much better than doing just one side.
3. Be sure to get all the corners and edges of the windows.
4. The brand-name glass cleaners aren't always the best. Buy a lesser known or generic brand and save money!

Yes!
I Do Windows!

I will wash your windows -
* Thoroughly
* Inside & out (if asked)
* Corner to corner and top to bottom
* I also do screens!

I can do what you know you hate to do . . . windows!

Call _____ at _____
for crystal clear windows all the time

5. This job has wide appeal. Don't just distribute flyers to homes. Contact local businesses or schools for work. They have windows too, and, most of the time, they have a lot more windows than a house (which means more money).

6. If you need a ladder to wash any windows, don't go on the top step, and be careful!!

suggested fees For an average household size window, charge between 40 and 60 cents per window. So, for example, if you charge 50 cents per window and you wash 20 windows, you make $10! For larger windows in business buildings and specially made homes, charge higher using your good judgment.

23
Decks & fences

You can earn big profits by tending to other people's decks and fences.

job description
Painting and/or water-sealing decks and fences.

qualifications
You must:

☆ Know how to use a paintbrush or roller brush efficiently
☆ Enjoy painting

target customers
All people with homes that have wooden decks or fences, local businesses with wooden decks or fences.

start-up costs
Duplication of flyers: $3.00 to $10.00; paintbrush: approximately $3.50; roller: approximately $4.00.

ideas for success
1. Use an up-and-down motion with your brush. Use enough paint to thoroughly cover the surface, but not too much that the paint drips or clumps.
2. Once you've established a pattern (up and down), don't change and go in a different direction, or the strokes will show up when the paint dries.
3. If the deck or fence is very large and the planks are extra wide, use a roller brush to save time. However, if the boards are thinner, use a brush because, if you don't, you'll get paint drops between the boards.
4. Apply at least two coats. The paint color will look richer, and the water seal will protect better.
5. Sweep decks free of all leaves, dust, and sticks before starting.

Deck & Fence Painting

Available

* I paint multiple coats.
* I water seal.
* I varnish or stain.
* I use the paint you've specified.

Let me save you time by tending to your decks and fences!

**Call _____ at _____
for all your deck and fence painting needs.**

6. There are many different kinds, qualities, and colors of paint and water sealant, and I suggest that you ask your clients to buy the paint or sealant so they get exactly what they want.

suggested fees   Estimate the number of hours it will take you to do the job and tell your client up front. Then let him or her make a decision. For a job of this nature, $7 to $10 per hour is reasonable.

24
Curb painting

How often have you been trying to find someone's house in an unfamiliar neighborhood and you can't find any addresses on the houses?

job description Painting house addresses on the curbs in front of houses to make them easier to identify.

qualifications You must be:

☆ Accurate with numbers
☆ Neat and meticulous

target customers Anyone who has an address!

start-up costs Duplication of flyers: $3 to $10; number stencils; spray paint: approximately $4.50 per can.

ideas for success
1. Contact the city engineering department or city hall to get the correct addresses of all the houses in your neighborhood.
2. A set of 4- to 5-inch-tall number stencils will make the job much easier.
3. Use black for the numbers and white for the background.
4. Make a template (stencil) for a plain white background for the numbers. Paint this on first, then paint the numbers over it.
5. Deliver the flyers at least a week before doing the job.

Dear Neighbor,

On _____, I will be painting addresses on the curb for every house in the neighborhood. Since this is for the convenience of you and others, I am only going to ask for donations for my service. After I perform this service, I will be by to collect any donation you feel is appropriate for this job. Thank you for your cooperation.

_____

6. Make a record of all the houses you deliver flyers to. You don't want to deliver a flyer then not paint their curb.
7. This is a very different type of job. Essentially, if you do one, you have to do them all. For this reason, the flyer and way you get paid is different. The flyer (which you're to deliver a week before) says that you'll be performing this service on whatever date. After you paint the address, go to the door, tell the person you did this service, and ask for donations. You might say something like, "I've painted your address on your curb for the convenience of others. Any donation you feel appropriate would be appreciated." Most people will give between $1 and $2.

suggested fees You should get paid on a donation basis, as previously described.

25
Mail retriever

With this job, you not only retrieve mail, but profits as well!

job description   Collecting mail at neighbors' houses every day while they're away on vacation. When they return, you give them all of their mail. This prevents mail theft and leaves room in the mailbox for a big batch of mail.

qualifications   You must be:

☆ Trustworthy
☆ Honest
☆ Able to work in all types of weather

target customers   Any neighbor or nearby resident who receives mail and takes vacations; the elderly; shut-ins who can't go outside to get their own mail.

start-up costs   Duplication of flyers: $3 to $10.

ideas for success

1. When your clients hire you to collect their mail, they're putting trust in you. They're trusting you to leave their mail for them to view. Don't go through, peek into, or even examine the envelopes in the mail. Mail is private, and you're being trusted to respect that.
2. Have a specific box or place where you put the mail each day and be sure you put it there. A lost piece of mail could be disastrous for your client.
3. When retrieving mail, have a bag to put it in, especially if you're riding your bike. This will make the mail easier to carry and eliminate the suspicions of people who pass you.

Are you going away on business or pleasure?

Through my:

Mail Retrieving Service

I can collect your mail for you while you're away.

* I come by every day and collect your mail so your mailbox doesn't overflow and so no one steals your mail.

* I am very responsible with your mail. I won't read or lose any of it.

* I respect your privacy.

* I'll bring your mail back to you as soon as you arrive home.

Call _____ at _____
for responsible mail retrieval

4. As soon as possible after your clients get back, arrange a time to return their mail to them. You don't want their mail hanging around your house unless necessary, and they'll want to receive it as quickly as possible.

suggested fees I would recommend 50 cents to $1.50 per day. So, for example, if your client were taking a two-week vacation and you were charging $1 per day, you'd make $14!

26
Grocery shopping

Ring up profits for yourself by shopping for others.

job description Shopping for people who don't have time or are unable to shop for themselves. Delivering the goods to your client's house.

qualifications You must be:

☆ Conscientious
☆ Capable of counting money
☆ Able to read
☆ Honest
☆ Capable of comparing values among competing products
☆ Familiar with the store layout
☆ Good in math

target customers The elderly, shut-ins who can't get supplies themselves, busy families, neighbors who don't have time to go shopping.

start-up costs Duplication of flyers: $3 to $10.

ideas for success

1. Have your clients make a complete list of everything they want. Have them specify on the list if they want a specific kind and size of something. For example: crackers—Ritz 16-ounce box. If it's not on the list, you don't get it.
2. Request that your client look through the daily newspaper for any coupons for items that they want. This will save them money.
3. Agree on a set time that you'll come to pick up the list and approximately the amount of money the groceries will cost. To verify the amount you received, write on the grocery list the exact amount of money your client gives you.

4. Deliver the groceries as soon as you're finished shopping. Get the groceries once a week, every five days, or whenever your client requests. Always show up at the agreed-upon time, unless otherwise specified by your client.
5. Notify your client at least a week in advance if you'll be unable to come at your given time so another time can be agreed on.
6. You'll need some form of transportation to and from the store. If it's convenient for them, go with your mother and father when they go shopping. While they're getting their things, you gather your things. Or, if there are only a few items, take a backpack and ride your bike.
7. While you're at the grocery store, be sure to add up the amount the groceries will cost you, and be sure you have enough money. You don't want to get to the checkout and not have enough money.

suggested fees I recommend that you charge $5 to $10 per time you shop. Upon delivering the groceries, give to your client the receipt and any change due. Collect the amount you've agreed upon for your pay.

Grocery Shopping Service

Don't have time or are unable to shop for your own groceries? I can help!

* I buy what is on <u>your</u> list.

* I shop for quality, yet I am price conscious.

* I can shop for you weekly, or whenever you need me.

* I deliver the groceries right to your door!

Let me save you time by doing your grocery shopping for you!

Call _____ **at** _____

for convenient and efficient shopping services.

27
Parent's helper

It's babysitting with a parent home!

job description
Entertaining children and keeping them out of the parent's way while he or she is home doing household chores like cooking and cleaning.

qualifications
You must be:

☆ Good with children
☆ Patient
☆ Understanding
☆ Fun-loving
☆ Responsible
☆ Open-minded and flexible

target customers
Parents who have young children.

start-up costs
Duplication of flyers: $3 to $10.

ideas for success
1. Before you show up for work, set up a time to meet and get to know the kids so that they and their parents are comfortable with you.
2. Don't be afraid to sit the child down if he or she is misbehaving.
3. Before the parent goes to work, discuss all activities that you may do with the children and their likes and dislikes. Once the parent begins work, he or she should be disturbed only when necessary.

Can't get any work done with your kids around?

While you work, let me entertain them as a

Parent's Helper

I play games, read, and have fun with your kids to free you up to do household things like cleaning, cooking, and working.

Don't let your kids prevent you
from getting things done . . .

Call _____ at _____
to give you some help with your kids!

4. When you're having problems with a child, consult the parent. He or she knows best!
5. Be aware of what the children aren't allowed to do. Kids can be pretty sneaky!
6. Remember, you're the boss.
7. Ask if the parent wants you to answer the phone or door, or if the parent will do it.
8. Don't give any medicine unless instructed by the parent.
9. Know whether you're responsible for preparing lunch and snacks, then discuss with the parent what's to be prepared.
10. Above all, have fun with the kids!

suggested fees This service is often more highly valued than babysitting! I would ask between $1 and $3 per child per hour. Discuss this with the parent.

28
Sign maker

For the creative person, signs are fun to make, and they're in demand by many people and organizations.

job description
Creating signs and posters for informative, decorative, or advertising purposes for others. Garage sales, group activities, or parties are a few popular occasions for using signs.

qualifications
You must:

☆ Be talented in art and layout
☆ Enjoy working with your hands

target customers
Special interest groups, small business owners, families who have parties or garage sales.

start-up costs
Duplication of flyers: $3 to $10. Set of markers, poster board, paper, additional supplies. You might already have many of these supplies, since you're an art lover.

ideas for success
1. Meet or talk with your client about things like the size of the signs, whether a specific layout is desired, what colors the sign should be, and any other special layout requirements.
2. Consult art, layout, and color books to improve your skill as a sign maker. You'll find many of these books available at your local library.
3. In some cases, rub-on or stick-on letters would be appropriate. These letters look very professional and are easy to apply. Your local art supply store should have a wide selection available.
4. Make the signs as colorful and eye-catching as possible. Use bright, coordinating colors. Make important words larger and more noticeable. To fill space, use small decorations relating to the topic. Be very neat; use rulers, compasses, and other drawing tools if available.

Custom-Made Signs

* Signs of all sizes

* Signs for all occasions

* Professional and creative

**Call _____ at _____
for eye-catching, creative and colorful signs.**

5. If you have a drawing talent, include drawings on the signs.
6. Always put a border around all signs.
7. In the bottom right-hand corner, sign your name and the present year.
8. When preparing signs, use any knowledge of special art techniques. These signs are your creations. Put yourself into them. Your knowledge might make your signs look 10 times better than the average sign.
9. Have a few examples of finished signs to show possible clients so they can see the quality of work they'll be getting.

suggested fees

Charge your client by the size of the poster you do. Have a list of various measurements and prices to choose from. I recommend starting your list with a 12-inch-by-15-inch sign priced between $4 and $7 per sign. Increase size and price from there. Be sure to take into account the costs of any materials you must purchase, such as rub-off letters. Costs of materials should be included in the price of the sign and still show a profit for you.

29
Party server

While serving hors d'oeuvres, food, and drinks, you'll be serving yourself profit!

job description Serving food, drinks, and appetizers at other people's parties. Cleaning up glasses and excess food when guests are finished.

qualifications You must be:

☆ Sociable and respectful
☆ Mature

target customers Neighbors who have parties or gatherings; local businesses, churches, and schools.

start-up costs Duplication of flyers: $3 to $10.

ideas for success
1. Dress accordingly, depending on what type of gathering it is. Find out from your client what kind of food and drink you'll be serving and about how many people will be there. Also find out if you'll be the only server there, or if there will be others helping you.
2. Practice balancing things on a tray at home, so you won't spill anything when you get there.
3. Arrive between 30 and 45 minutes early to get everything ready and to get used to where you'll be serving.
4. Negotiate specific hours ahead of time. If the party runs over the designated time, you might not want to stick around that long.

Having a party?

Need help with . . .
Party Serving?

Give me a call!

* I serve food, appetizers, entrees and whatever else you have.

* I am responsible and polite.

* I am mature and respectful.

* I'll help make your party run as smoothly as possible.

Call _____ at _____
for polite and respectful party serving.

suggested fees You should get paid by the hour for this one. It's honest because you only stay as long as your client needs you. I would charge $2 to $4 per hour.

30
Tutor/musical instructor

Have you ever heard of studying yourself sick? Well, study yourself to more money!

job description Helping someone study for school or other activities. Providing extra help in a certain area as a tutor. Serving as a private instructor for your musical instrument.

qualifications You must:

★ Be a fairly good student
★ Do well or have lots of knowledge about a certain subject or instrument
★ Be patient
★ Have extra time that won't interfere with your own studies

target customers School students of all ages, adults taking college courses.

start-up costs Duplication of flyers: $3 to $10.

ideas for success
1. Be sure you have a complete understanding of the subject you're tutoring.
2. It's a good idea to tutor someone younger than you. They'll respect you more that way.
3. Arrange a meeting place (your home or your student's) and agree on a set time of the day or week to tutor your student. Be sure the location is quiet and will be free of interruptions. Always come at the set time unless otherwise agreed upon by both of you.

Available

Academic Tutor

Having problems with school?

Do you need that extra bit of special help?

Let me help!

The way I see it, we have to be in school, so why not do the best you can? I can help you do just that!

I am good in the areas of:

_____

_____

Call _____ at _____

for academic help that can make your school year better.

Available

Musical Tutor

Having problems with your _____?

Do you need that extra bit of special help?

Let me help! I am an experienced player of _____ years and am interested in seeing you succeed with your instrument.

I love music and want to help you to love it too!

Call _____ at _____

for a musical tutor who can help you become the best you can be.

4. Be patient. Your student might not understand something as well as you do and it might take time, but that's what you're there for.

5. A very popular type of tutoring is private musical instrument lessons. So if you play an instrument well, inform your instructor that you can teach privately and the instructor will let her less-talented students know (also give the teacher some flyers to pass out).

6. If you have to cancel an appointment, let your student know well ahead of time so another time can be worked out.

7. Tutoring doesn't mean giving answers. It means helping your student understand the concepts necessary to get the answers. If you just give answers, you can be accused of cheating.

suggested fees Charge your student by the hour. Most study periods last about an hour. Charge somewhere between $5 and $10 per hour.

31
Handyperson's helper

Many more people are doing building and repairs on their own homes, but who will be there to hold the ladder? You!

job description Assisting people with repair or construction work by doing things like holding ladders, passing and assembling tools, hammering nails, or any other help your client might need.

qualifications You must:

- ☆ Know which tools are which and how to use them
- ☆ Be a safety-minded person
- ☆ Be responsible and trustworthy
- ☆ Be patient and cooperative
- ☆ Know and use teamwork
- ☆ Have basic repair knowledge

target customers Handypeople you know such as neighbors or relatives looking to do home repairs or improvements now or in the future.

start-up costs Duplication of flyers: $3 to $10. You'll be using your client's tools and materials.

ideas for success
1. Before you begin work, get to know the client you'll be working with. This job takes teamwork and cooperation, which comes easier if you know the person.
2. Learn the names, danger areas, and proper uses of all common tools. This will make it easier on you and your client.
3. Holding a ladder doesn't mean standing on it. Plant two feet on the ground and hold the ladder firmly with two hands.
4. Listen to and obey all instructions and suggestions from your client. This is his or her project. You're just there to help.

Handyperson's Helper

Available

I do everything, from holding ladders to handing you tools.

If by chance some unforeseen accident occurs (heaven forbid!), I'll be there to scrape you off the pavement.

You only have 2 hands, but I have two more!

Call _____ at _____
for help with the simplest or most involved home repair and improvement projects.

5. If you have a suggestion or comment, by all means, say it, but at the proper time and with respect.
6. Check with your client before you do something on your own. The client might have a certain way he or she wants things done, or what you're doing might be wrong.
7. Always stick close to your client (except when given special instructions). You never know when the client might need you.
8. Don't play around on the job.
9. In a job like this, and all jobs for that matter, safety comes first. You're there to help, but if your client has to repeatedly keep you from doing unsafe things—you won't be much help!

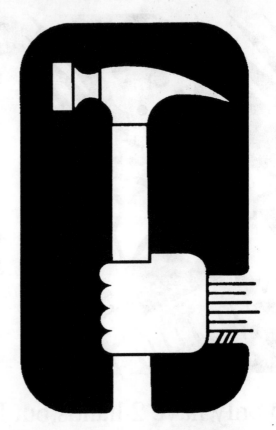

suggested fees Since you're working on your client's time, charge by the hour for this one. Charge between $2 and $4 per hour.

32
Paper-route fill-in

An old-fashioned job with a new twist! Not having the job full-time gives you money and freedom.

job description Filling in for kids who have a full-time paper route but are on vacation, sick, or really busy.

qualifications You must:

☆ Have access to a bike and be able to ride it
☆ Be trustworthy
☆ Be honest

target customers Kids with paper routes.

start-up costs Duplication of flyers: $3 to $10.

ideas for success
1. Meet with your client before he or she goes away. Have the client make out a list or map of all the houses that should be delivered to. Have the client include the address of each house. Also ask if there's a special place a certain person likes the paper delivered: in the mailbox or on the porch, for example.
2. Get complete instructions from your client as to exactly what you're to do and how you're to do it.
3. Don't walk in anyone's yard. Use driveways, streets, and sidewalks.
4. You might also have to fold the papers before you deliver them. Ask your client how to do this.
5. Use your bike, or, if you can drive, your car to deliver the papers. If it's raining, have something to protect the papers, or ask your parents to drive you. If anyone of the subscribers has a message for your client, write it down and keep it until you see the client again.

Need someone to fill in for your paper route while you are gone? Call me!

Paper Route Fill-In

* Whenever you need me,
I'll be there:
illness, vacation,
too much homework, etc.

* I'm a responsible and
reliable fill-in.

No person will go without a paper when I'm filling in!

Call _____ at _____
anytime you need a fill-in for your paper route.

suggested
fees This all depends on what the client makes per delivery. Discuss this with the client and agree on a fee. If you have to perform an extra service such as folding or collecting money, add on to your fee accordingly.

33
Designing jewelry

You can make and sell beautiful jewelry. Once you get started, you'll even be able to design several pieces of your own.

job description Making jewelry sets (including earrings and a necklace) and selling them at fairs, stores, door-to-door, or at social gatherings.

qualifications You must:

☆ Be creative
☆ Enjoy making things
☆ Be patient
☆ Work well with your hands
☆ Be "crafty"

target customers People who like to wear jewelry or give jewelry as presents.

start-up costs Duplication of flyers: $3 to $10. Materials: approximately $5 to $20.

ideas for success

1. Deliver the flyers, then three to four days later, go to each house you delivered a flier to and talk to the owners. Show the owners a sample of what you're selling and give them another flier if needed. They might even buy some on the spot.
2. Set up a table or agree with another group to rent or borrow part of their booth at fairs, malls, and social events such as school fund-raisers or parties.
3. Talk to local jewelry or department stores. They might buy your jewelry to sell in their stores.
4. Ask your mom or dad to take some pieces to where they work. Many of their coworkers might be interested.

suggested fees Charge for each piece of jewelry. I recommend charging between $6 and $8 for a pair of large earrings and between $5 and $7 for the smaller ones. Charge between $8 and $10 for the large necklace, and $7 to $9 for the small one. Or have a combined rate of between $14 and $18 for both large pieces and between $12 and $16 for the small set. Encourage your customers to buy a full set because if you're selling more jewelry, you can afford to give the customers a small discount this way. Since they're saving money, they might buy both pieces.

materials The following materials will make one large and one small necklace and one large and one small pair of earrings.

☆ Seven 1½-inch-by-⅝-inch oval wooden shapes
☆ Seven ⅞-inch-by-⅜-inch oval wooden shapes
☆ Six ¾-inch-diameter circular wooden shapes
☆ Six ⅜-inch-diameter circular wooden shapes
☆ Teal powdered glitter
☆ Fuchsia powdered glitter
☆ White iridescent powdered glitter
☆ Three 30-inch strands of ¹⁄₁₆-inch-wide mauve flat metallic ribbon
☆ Three 25-inch strands of ¹⁄₁₆-inch-wide mauve flat metallic ribbon
☆ Two 1½-inch strands of ¹⁄₁₆-inch-wide mauve flat metallic ribbon
☆ Two 1½-inch strands of ¹⁄₁₆-inch-wide blue flat metallic ribbon
☆ Six deep blue 8mm-by-4mm navette beads
☆ One 4-inch square piece of thin cardboard
☆ Glue
☆ One popsicle stick
☆ Four earring backs
☆ Spray fixative (I used Blair Spray Fixative.)

instructions 1. Prepare the shapes. For my jewelry, I used precut wooden pieces for the shapes. These can be found at local craft shops.
2. Put glitter on the shapes. I used fuchsia, teal, and white for my jewelry. You can use whatever colors you want. The colors could also be changed around and put in different configurations to form the jewelry. We'll put glitter on all the shapes at once, then put them all together. On a scrap piece of paper, put a good sized glob of glue. Fold your piece of cardboard in half and place it on the table. This is to catch the

For Sale!

Beautiful
Jewelry

The perfect gift for any occasion

A set of earrings and a necklace available

For Sale individually or together

Only _____ each or _____ for both

Call _____ at _____ for more information
or samples of this jewelry

extra glitter that falls so you can reuse it. With a popsicle stick, put a thin coat of glue on one side. Then, lightly tap glitter from the container onto the glued surface. Do this over your cardboard so you catch the extra glitter. Tap off the excess glitter onto the cardboard. When you're all finished, use the cardboard to pour the extra glitter back into the container. Now comes the toughest part. Lightly holding the wooden shape between your thumb and forefinger, spread glue onto the edges of the shape and dip the glued edges into the pile of glitter. Then set it aside on a napkin or piece of paper to dry. When dry, spread glue and add glitter to the other side. Set aside to dry overnight. Repeat this process with all of your other shapes until all of them are covered with glitter. Remember, you can gently hold the glittered portions of your shapes in order to cover the other sides with glue. However, don't rub the glittered portions off! Cover the following number of shapes with the listed colors of powdered glitter:

- Large ovals: four teal, two white, one fuchsia
- Large circles: four fuchsia, one white, one teal
- Small ovals: two teal, three fuchsia, two white
- Small circles: three teal, two fuchsia, one white

3. Seal the shapes. Lay the shapes out on a newspaper outside the house. Use the spray fixative and spray the pieces on both sides with a good coat. This will eliminate the problem of glitter shedding and falling off.

4. Assemble the earrings. I'll explain how to assemble the large earrings. Follow this same process for making the small earrings, excluding the bead at the top. (Follow the figure below for placement assistance.) Glue one circle, overlapping the top of the oval. Glue the strands of ribbon diagonally across the bottom of the oval. Wrap the ends around the back and glue them down. Use the shortest ribbon lengths and alternate colors of ribbon and glitter. Glue the navette bead to the center of the circle. It might slide, so hold it for a minute or so. (Don't add beads on the small set of earrings.) Turn the earring over. On the very tip of the oval that's under the circle shape, glue the earring back in place. Add enough glue to hold the backing on. Let dry overnight. Repeat this process for the other large earring and the set of small earrings.

5. Assemble the necklace. I arranged shapes for my necklace in a way I liked. If you want to use my configuration, see below. If not, arrange your shapes in whatever way you'd like. I made a base with all of the ovals first. Then I added the circles on top. The one important thing to remember is to start from the bottom and work up. When you're all finished placing and gluing your shapes, add the four oval-shaped beads onto the four circles for the larger necklace only. Then set to dry overnight. Repeat this process, or your own configuration, when making the small necklace.

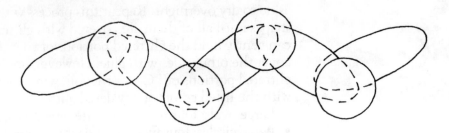

6. Attach the necklace tie. Once your necklace shape has dried, you need to give it a string tie. Take your three strands of 30-inch metallic ribbon and tie a knot 1½ inch from one end. Then either tape that end to a table or have a partner hold it and braid the three strands. When done, knot the other end. Fold the braided ribbon in half to find the midpoint, and glue this point to the center spot on the back of the wooden necklace. Glue the rest of the ribbon down as straight as possible on the back of the necklace and let it dry. Repeat this process for the small necklace, using the 24-inch lengths of ribbon.

34
Worms for fishing

With the worms you collect, you can really cast off and reel in some big profits!

job description Digging up buckets of worms for people who like to fish.

qualifications You must:

☆ Like working in dirt
☆ Not be afraid to touch those slimy, icky worms

target customers Neighbors, friends, and family who like to go fishing.

start-up costs Styrofoam cups: 49 cents for 50; trowel, tinfoil, rubber bands.

ideas for success
1. Be sure the place you dig for worms is okay to dig in. Don't go digging up your front yard!
2. The best time to get worms is right after a rainstorm. The soil is easy to dig in, and lots of worms are near the surface. Worms might also be lying on the pavement after a storm.
3. Put your worms in styrofoam cups. Put about 25 worms in one cup. Fill the rest of the cup up with dirt so the worms can stay alive before the fisher uses them.
4. Be sure the worms are a decent size. Don't sell little dinky worms that probably can't even be put on a hook! Catch them big!
5. Check with local sporting goods stores for suggestions on where to find and sell good worms.
6. Deliver flyers to local sports supply stores. Perhaps they'll want to buy worms from you to sell to their customers.

Hey, Anglers!

Do you need bait for your next outing?
I'll dig up all the . . .

WORMS. . .

. . . you need, cheaper that any bait shop!

As many worms as you
need - I'll dig them
for you!

Save time and money!

Make the most out of
your fishing trip with
fresh, quality worms!

Call _____ at _____
for worms for your next fishing trip.

7. Find out where most local residents fish. Get up early and pass out flyers, or set up a table there.
8. Cover each cup with tinfoil and a rubber band to shelter it from the heat and air. If not, you'll fry the worms!

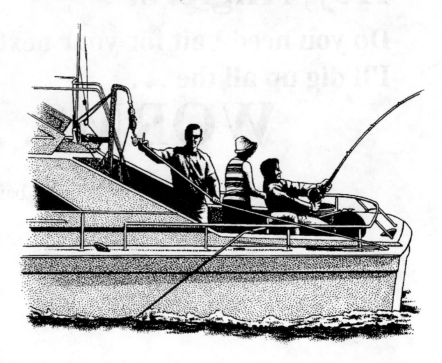

suggested fees As described above, package 25 worms per styrofoam cup and charge your clients per cup. Charge between $2 and $3 for each cup.

35
Stick-&-branch cleanup

Storms can be pretty damaging. They also leave behind lots of debris and sticks that were blown over. Pick these up and pick up profits at the same time.

job description
Picking up any sticks, branches, or other debris from your client's yard after storms or high winds, and disposing of the debris properly.

qualifications
You must:

☆ Be unafraid of work
☆ Have no problem bending over repeatedly
☆ Be thorough

target customers
Property owners who live by trees, and owners of large buildings (apartments and businesses) who have trees on or near their lot.

start-up costs
Duplication of flyers: $3 to $10. Your own hands: free!

ideas for success
1. Deliver flyers to local businesses and apartment buildings as well as homes.
2. Once sticks are collected, you can either dump them in a wooded lot (no one else's property), bundle them up and give them to your client as kindling (small wood used to start fires), or, in some communities, sticks can be put out with the trash. Ask your local trash collector.
3. Be thorough; get all the sticks off the ground, not just the really big ones.
4. A big bag might be helpful in gathering the smaller sticks before disposing of them.

Available

Stick-and-Branch Cleanup Services

* I clean up your messy yard after storms, winds, natural disasters, and anything else that might come your way.

* After I'm done with your yard, you won't even be able to tell that it <u>ever</u> was a mess!

**Call _____ at _____
the next time a storm makes a mess of your yard!**

suggested fees The basic rate should be determined by the size of the yard. Charge between $4 and $8 per half acre of yard (see chapter 18, Leaf raking) or talk to your client about specific fees based on an estimate of how many sticks you have to pick up.

36
Trash collector

While collecting other people's trash, you'll also be collecting heavy profits.

job description Carrying trash down to the street. Taking any trash cans back up from the street after the trash has been picked up.

qualifications You must:

☆ Be fairly strong
☆ Not mind a little "dirty" work
☆ Be responsible

target customers Anyone who has trash to take out; older or disabled people who can't take the trash out themselves or need help doing it.

start-up costs Duplication of flyers: $3 to $10.

ideas for success
1. Before starting your job, speak with your client about several things. First, find out what day the trash company collects your client's trash. Write this down so you won't forget. Then see when your client wants you to take care of the trash (for example, the night before or that morning). Also ask when your client wants you to take the trash cans back up. To your client, this is very important. Go over everything beforehand so there are no questions.
2. Always show up at your designated time. If you have a conflict, talk to your client ahead of time.
3. Don't forget to come back later in the day to take the cans back up to your client's house.

Do you need a . . .

Trash Collector?

Call me!

* I don't mind a little dirty work!

* Leave your bagged trash by your door and I will carry the trash down to the street to be collected.

* I will come back later and bring your trash cans back up from the street.

Call _____ at _____
to take care of all your trash needs.

suggested fees For the service of taking the trash down to the street each week, choose one of two fees: one fee per bag or one fee per can. I recommend between 25 cents and 50 cents per bag and 75 cents and $1 per can. (If you do this every week, it starts to add up!) Remember, the fee per can includes taking it back up from the street later in the day.

37
Decorate clothing

You can decorate and sell all types of clothing, including hats, shirts, pants, and shoes.

qualifications   You must:

☆ Be patient
☆ Enjoy creating your own designs

target customers   Anyone who likes to wear decorated clothing or needs gifts for others.

start-up costs   Duplication of flyers: $3 to $10. Available materials include fabric paints, beads, trimmings, and others that are too numerous to list. Just be sure your selling price is greater than the total cost of materials.

ideas for success
1. Be on the lookout for specific clothing decorations that are popular in your area. These might include paints and beads. Also be on the lookout for brushes and clothes to decorate.
2. You can find many materials at local craft stores or department stores.
3. Visit local craft or fabric stores and ask for the wearable art department. In this area, you'll find lots of ideas and supplies for decorating: booklets, project sheets, videos, in-store models, and on-package designs.
4. Stay flexible and get those creative juices flowing.

For Sale!

Creative Different Imaginative Original

Clothing Designs

* Attractive, washable designs
  painted on clothing by me!

* Designs on shirts, pants, shoes,
  hats, and more!

* Personalized designs available!

* Clothing for special occasions!

* I make house calls to show you
  what you are getting!

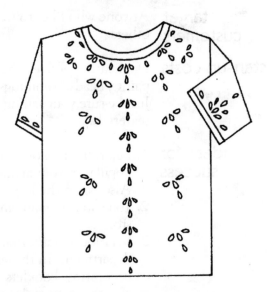

Call _____ at _____ with
questions or orders for original clothing designs!

suggested fees Be sure you figure all your costs into the final selling price of your piece of clothing. Then add an extra fee for profit and your work. This can range from $2 to $10 extra; it all just depends on how much time and labor are involved in creating the design.

38
Light housekeeping

By doing light cleaning for other people, you'll clean up on profits.

job description
Doing light cleaning jobs such as sweeping and washing floors, washing windows, dusting, washing dishes, shaking out rugs, and trash collecting. You can provide these services for people's homes, gathering places, and places of business.

qualifications
You must:

☆ Be a thorough and complete worker
☆ Know how to use basic cleaning equipment
☆ Be reliable
☆ Enjoy cleaning

target customers
Busy families who don't have time to clean (or families with small children); elderly people who can't clean their own houses; building and meeting-hall owners.

start-up costs
Duplication of flyers: $3 to $10. No other costs, unless you provide the cleaning equipment (see the following).

ideas for success
1. The best way to handle equipment (brooms, vacuums, chemical cleaners, etc.) is to have your clients provide the necessities. This way, they'll be able to get the kind they want you to use. If your clients want you to provide the equipment, discuss this with them. This will be included in your start-up costs and should be appropriately added to your final fee.
2. Several of the other jobs described in this book could be added to these services. For example, window washing and trash collecting. (See those descriptions for more detail.)

Is your house in need of a little tidying?
If so, call me for . . .

Light
House-Cleaning Services

* I'll take care of the little
  things around your
  house that you don't
  have time for!

* I wash dishes, sweep
  floors, clean, and more!

* Any other small request?
  I'll do it!

I can save you time by helping out around your house

**Call _____ at _____
for more info about my light house cleaning services!**

3. It's very important in this job to be thorough in your work. Clean everything. Don't forget corners or really dirty areas. Remember, the better job you do now, the more likely you are to be asked back again.

4. Be on time. Show up to clean when your clients expect you to be there. Their house might be so dirty that it couldn't stand to go another day without being cleaned. If you can't be there on time, talk to your clients.

5. Don't just clean around things; move them and clean underneath.

6. Talk to your clients ahead of time. Discuss exactly what you're to clean, when and how often you're to clean, and any specific instructions your clients might have.

7. Follow to the letter all requests and directions given by your clients. It's better to cooperate than miscommunicate.

suggested fees It's best to charge by the hour for this job. However, work efficiently and diligently and don't take advantage of the hourly rate. If you take too long and don't do a good enough job, you won't be asked back. I recommend charging between $4 and $5 per hour.

39
Cooking for neighbors

By cooking for neighbors, you can also cook up some profits.

job description
Preparing meals for your neighbors. This includes cooking, table setting, and serving. Cleanup after the meal is a service you could offer to your clients, but it's not necessary.

qualifications
You must be:

☆ A good cook
☆ Reliable and on time
☆ Efficient

target customers
Families with two working parents; single-parent homes; families with many younger kids; elderly people who can't cook for themselves; sick persons who just need a nice bowl of chicken soup now and then.

start-up costs
Duplication of flyers: $3 to $10. Costs will vary greatly, depending on what food you buy. All food purchased for meals will be included in start-up costs and should be added to your fee accordingly (see the following).

ideas for success
1. Make a menu of a variety of dinners that you know how to make (look through recipe books for more ideas). Include at least 20 dinners that your client can choose from according to the likes and dislikes of the family. Sit down with your client and plan what you'll make for the entire week. This way you'll have time to buy groceries for the dinners. Also discuss the portion sizes to make.
2. This job could be combined with grocery shopping (see chapter 26).
3. Since you know what you'll make and what supplies are needed, it's best for you to buy the necessary groceries for each meal. Ask your client if a certain brand is preferred. If not, shop

Don't have time to cook? Let Me!

Cooking Services

* I'll come over before you get home to cook you and your family a nice hot meal.

* You have many dinner options. I cook to please!

* I clean up my cooking mess when I'm done so you can have a quiet dinner together with your family.

You'll walk into your house to the smell of a hot, home-cooked meal!

**Call _____ at _____
for more info about my cooking services.**

efficiently. Just because it's the most expensive, that doesn't mean it's the best!

4. Discuss timing with your client. Based on what time the client gets home, you have to take the responsibility for going to the house in time to prepare the meal before the client gets home. If you're late, you inconvenience your client. This is a job where being on time is almost as important as your cooking.

5. Important: Clean up all the messes you make while cooking. You don't want your client coming home to a hot meal and a messy kitchen. Again, it inconveniences your client. You made the mess, you clean it up!!

6. Put any food you don't use in the refrigerator for future use. There's no sense in wasting food.

7. Don't burn the food!

suggested fees Charge a flat rate per meal of $10 to $15 for up to 3 hours of work. If the meal takes longer than that, adjust accordingly. Also add in all your expenses in buying groceries to make the meal. For example: if you bought $25 worth of groceries and charge a $12 flat rate, you'd make $37 per meal (part of this goes towards buying groceries for the next meal). You can also ask for an advance amount of money from your client to buy groceries. Your client might also want to purchase supplies themselves. Then you need to just prepare them.

40
Plant sitting

By tending to other people's plants, you'll tend to profits for yourself.

job description
Frequently watering and taking care of plants while their owners are out of town. Maintaining plants in businesses, offices, or meeting buildings.

qualifications
You must be:

☆ Reliable
☆ Responsible

target customers
Neighbors and friends who have plants in their house. Local businesses and office buildings that have plants in the building.

start-up costs
Duplication of flyers: $3 to $10. Watering can: $5 to $8.

ideas for success
1. Don't forget to show up when you're supposed to. Talk with your client about when and how often he or she wants you to maintain the plants. Remember, if you forget to do your job, the plants might die.
2. Don't water too much. You'll drown the plants.
3. Ask your client about any special instructions regarding treatment of plants. For example: Watering on the leaves of a violet flower is not recommended.
4. If the plant has begun to bend or lean to face the sun, turn it around to even its growth.

Available Plant Sitter

* I'll take care of all your plants' needs while you are away.

* I am a responsible, reliable person and will not forget about your plants' important needs.

* I take care of all plants, from a small pot of ivy greens to palm trees!

Leave your plants in my reliable hands!

Call _____ at _____
take care of all your plants' needs while you are away

suggested fees For this job, charge per plant per day. I recommend between 25 cents and 50 cents per day.

41
The business side

Having your own small business enables you to make money. However, in order to continue that business and keep it successful, there are many more factors involved. Good business practices such as accurate record keeping, reasonable prices, maintaining a budget, and responsibility with the money you make are all essential to keeping your business alive and organized. In this chapter, I focus on each of these wise business practices; I also highlight special business and money words used in this book, and I give you business tips based on my experiences with making money.

determining fees A *fee* is a certain dollar amount you charge to perform a certain job or service. Determining a reasonable fee can be very important to the success of your business. If you choose a fee that's too high, no one will hire you. However, if your fee is too low, you might end up losing money or not getting what you really deserve for a job. For these reasons, you should carefully consider each of the following fee guidelines to reasonably come up with a fee that's good for you and good for those you work for.

There are four main guidelines for determining fees:

1. Initial expenses
2. Amount of work done
3. The going rate in your area
4. Profit

By combining these guidelines, arriving at a fee is as easy as 1, 2, 3 . . . 4! Here's how:

1. Initial expenses. Most of the jobs in this book require a small amount of initial investment in order to start. All of these costs are covered in the start-up costs section of each job. These costs

are usually minimal, but nevertheless, they're money. You can obtain this money in several different ways. The best place to get it is from yourself. Maybe you have some money put away in a bank or at home in a "cookie jar." If you have enough, use it because you won't have to pay anyone back. If this is not possible, ask your parents or other close relative if you can borrow the money. Assure them that you'll pay them back as soon as you begin to make money. It's important to pay off your debts as soon as possible so you can begin keeping the money for yourself. Plus, you'll build a good reputation so that the next time you need to borrow money, they'll give it to you gladly.

2. Amount of work you do. Correctly figuring in the amount of work you do is crucial to your fee. For example, you wouldn't charge the same amount for mowing a half-acre yard and mowing a ten-acre yard!

3. Going rate. A *going rate* is an average fee that others in your area are getting paid to do the same job you do. For example, if you know that the going rate for walking dogs in your area is $3 per dog, it would be very unwise to charge $5 per dog, because obviously people would rather pay $3 than $5. So, if possible, charge the same as or even slightly lower than the average going rate (for example: $2.75 instead of $3.00). In the long run, even though you're charging less per dog, you'll make more money because more people will want to hire you at your low fee. You can find out what the going rate is in your area by asking friends who do the same job or by asking people who have hired others to do the job.

4. Profit. There's a simple formula that easily explains the concept of profit. It is:

Profit = Income (Sales) – Expenses (Costs)

Profit is the money left over after all your expenses are paid. Profit's the money you get to keep. Even though this might seem a bit confusing, it's all simplified in the suggested fees section of every job. This section gives a range of fees that are reasonable for that job. However, in order to come up with an exact fee to charge your customers, you'll have to consider the four preceding guidelines as they apply to you. The range is there to help you, and by consulting this section, determining fees is a snap!

record keeping When starting your own business, you naturally hope that you'll get lots of jobs fast. Hopefully, this will happen, but the more jobs you get, the harder it will be to remember who you worked for at a certain time, what you did for them, and how much you made. That's why it's very important to keep accurate and up-to-date records of your business. After completing each job, record all specific information about that job. The further you get away from the job, the harder it is to remember specifics. There are several things that should be recorded about each job. These things include who you performed that job for, what you did for them, the date, total income, total expenses, and profit. The best way to keep records of this sort would be a chart. Below is a copy of the chart I use when recording information about my jobs.

CLIENT	JOB PERFORMED	DATE	INCOME	EXPENSES	PROFIT
Mrs. Smith	Raked Leaves	1/25/92	$15.00	------	$15.00
Mr. Jones	Planned Birthday	10/18/92	$90.00	$45.00	$45.00

Records like this are best kept in a regular spiral notebook so they're all together. Simply draw the chart on the first few pages. When those are used up, do a few more, and so on. Don't get behind on your record keeping. The further away you get from a job, the harder it is to remember the details about it. The better records you keep, the more you'll be in tune with the progress of your business.

It's also very important to keep accurate information about every one of your clients. Records like this can be kept on a plain 3-by-5 index card. The first time you work with a new client, get the following information for your records:

- ☆ First and last name
- ☆ Address
- ☆ Phone number
- ☆ Specific information about the job you're doing for them. For example, if you babysit for them, include the names and ages of their children. Or if you rake leaves, the size of their yard.

Shown below is a sample of a card I use to keep track of my clients. Use a separate card for each client. Store the cards in a small box, but keep it handy. You never know when you'll need to get in touch with someone.

JOHN & KATHY WISE   ph# 492-1234
7764 Main Street NW
North Canton, OH   44720

Lindsay: Age 7   Johnathan: Age 3

---

handling the profits

Earlier in this chapter, I discussed the idea of profit. Before continuing with this section, it's important to realize the difference between the total amount of money you make and the amount of profit you generate. Refer to the previous section on determining fees if you have any questions about this.

Being paid for a job is a very good feeling, but before you get all excited about the amount you have, you must figure out how much money is actually yours. The first thing you must do when you get paid is to cover your expenses. For example, if you spend $43 on food and supplies for a birthday you planned and you got paid $95, then $43.00 of that must go to pay for your expenses. Therefore, you then have $52.00 profit that you can spend! If you do a job that has no expenses, all the money you get paid is yours.

The best way to handle the money you make is by having a "percentage plan." Before you begin your business, set percentages of your earnings for certain uses. For example, you might want to save or put in the bank 50 percent of the money, give 10 percent to school or church organizations, and keep 40 percent for your use. Or perhaps you might save 50 percent and keep 50 percent for your use. You'll have to decide on the specific percentages according to how you want to spend your money.

Because this aspect of your business is so important, I want to share with you a wonderful piece of advice given to me by my dad. He said that even though it's important to save money, pay yourself first. So that's my message to you. Always save a portion of it, but take some of it and spend it on the things you really want. After all, that's why you started your business in the first place, isn't it?

saving money One option you have with your money is to save it. However, the question is where and how to save it. Some people use the "cookie jar" method (saving it all in a jar or box at home). However, this is definitely not the best way to save. I suggest that you keep a little money at home for emergencies, and put the rest into a savings account at your local bank.

opening a bank account Opening your own savings account is fairly easy. It's the safest and securest place for your money to be. You'll be able to get to it if you need it, and by keeping it in a bank, you'll actually make more money!

To start your own account, first talk it over with your parents. One of your parents will have to go with you to the bank to cosign your account. Cosigning means they have to sign all the same papers you do because they're an adult. In some states, banking laws require minors (people under 18) to have all bank accounts in both their name and the name of one of their parents. Be sure you know, or have with you, your social security number and your home address. Tell one of the bank officials that you want to start your own account. They'll sit down with you and get all the necessary information. You'll have to sign a signature card so that no one but you (and your parents) can add or withdraw money to the account. Any other requirements will be taken care of by the bank official. With this account you'll be able to put in or take out money at any time. All accounts have a certain amount of interest paid to you every month. The interest is a percentage of the amount of money in your account. As the amount of money in your account grows, so will the interest.

Remember to use your money wisely. Always save. However, pay yourself first!

42
Advertising

Much of the success of your business will depend on your advertising and how you choose to do it. How will you get your business known and bring in more customers, and how will you keep the customers you've already worked with? People usually don't just come to you for services. You have to take some kind of initiative to communicate with your customers. In this book, I've included one form of advertising (flyers) for your use. In this chapter, I'll explain how to use the included flyers, some other possible forms of advertising that you could use, and how to keep the customers you already have.

how to use the flyers in this book

For each job in this book, I've included a graphically illustrated, complete, and comprehensive flyer that you can use to advertise your business. These flyers may be photocopied directly from the book for your use. However, before you crank out a whole bunch, you'll have to make a few "personal" adjustments to these flyers to make them yours. Here's what to do.

First, make one photocopy of the flyer that corresponds to the job you're doing. Then, on this copy, fill in the spaces for your name and phone number. For the jobs that require your potential customers to know more about you than just your name (such as babysitting), I've left several blanks for you to fill in your name and a few things about yourself to reinforce that you're a responsible and active person. (See my babysitting flyer in chapter 1.) If it's possible to type your information onto the flyer, do so. That will make it look consistent with the rest of the flyer. If not, write very neatly in ink. Once you've typed or written in the appropriate information, photocopy this flyer, making as many copies as you need. The size of the flyers is less than the size of a standard piece of paper. When you're finished copying, you might want to cut off the extra white space around the edges. Some copiers also enlarge copies, so you could enlarge the flyer to make it standard size. Also, remember to always make an extra copy for yourself that won't get delivered, in case you need to make more.

Now you have to deliver the flyers. Chances are, you're only going to be delivering them to houses in your own neighborhood, so putting flyers in the mail will be a waste of money. Delivering them by hand will save money, make sure they get to their destination, and it shouldn't take too long. So, on your bike or just walking, deliver your flyers to as many houses as possible. As you're delivering, analyze who you're delivering the flyers to. If you know that a certain family definitely can't use your service, don't put a flyer in that mailbox. For example, if you have an older couple living on your street, chances are they're not going to need babysitting services. While you're delivering, keep accurate records of every house you delivered a flyer to, for your own reference. Record the address and, if you know who lives there, the name.

Now that you've delivered all of your flyers, they're in the hands of your potential customers, and you have to wait. Hopefully, you'll have as much success with your flyers as I did with mine. I've found that many of my clients were so impressed with the professional look and completeness of my flyers that they hired me just for that reason. However, if your business is having trouble getting off the ground after a month or two, deliver another round of flyers to the same people, just to remind them. Your persistence and dedication will most likely pay off later on.

other forms of advertising

In addition to the flyers, the following are some other forms of advertising you could use to further promote your business.

phone soliciting

This is a popular form of advertising and often gets mixed results. Phone soliciting is basically calling potential customers to promote your business. When you call, sound polite and businesslike. These could be customers you're talking to, so you want to sound your best. Begin the conversation with "hello" and your name and age. Then, perhaps ask a question that could lead into your job. For example, if you're offering babysitting services, ask something like, "Do you have young children at home?" If the answer is yes, you could lead into another question like, "Are you ever in need of a babysitter?" Then go into explaining your job and a little about yourself. For most jobs, people won't hire you on the spot, but you're just reminding them that you're there. As they get to know you, they'll be more comfortable hiring you. Always end the conversation with a comment like, "Thank you for your time. Good-bye."

door-to-door This type of advertising is more for when you're selling a product or something you made (like the potpourri hearts or jewelry in this book), but door-to-door advertising could also be used to promote a service. This involves going up to people's doors and telling them about your product or service. Again, introduce yourself with your name and age. Then politely explain your service or show your product. Depending on what your job is, they might even hire you on the spot. If they don't, thank them for their time and give them a flyer to remember you by.

There are two major advantages of door-to-door advertising. First, if you're selling a product, it allows people to actually see what they're buying. I've specifically suggested door-to-door advertising for a few jobs. Door-to-door advertising also allows your potential customers to see you. With phone soliciting, they only hear you, and with flyers, they only see what your job is. By coming to their door, you let them know who will be working for them or who made these things.

word-of-mouth Word-of-mouth is probably the most important of the three forms of advertising that I've discussed. Word-of-mouth simply means that people, such as your clients, family, and friends, tell others about your service. People hearing of your service from other people that they know and trust can often have more credibility than if you advertise the job yourself.

There are a few things you can do to enhance your word-of-mouth advertising. First, ask your family, friends, and clients to tell people about your business. It doesn't take much effort on their part, and I'm sure they won't mind at all helping a family member or friend. Second, by advertising with flyers, phone solicitation, and door-to-door, you plant the information about your service into the minds of your potential customers. If the subject comes up, they might just remember about you and tell their friends. Third, when you perform your job or service, do a good job. If you perform your job well, you'll impress your client. If the client's impressed, he or she will be more inclined to tell other people about you.

Here's another tip for successful client relations. Send personalized letters to established customers. If someone has been hiring you often or even a few times, send a letter or a card to them at special times, like the holidays. Or just send a card at any time. This is simply a kind gesture that makes your client feel good and remember you.

Index